While every precaution has been taken in the preparation of this book, the publisher assumes no responsibility for errors or omissions, or for damages resulting from the use of the information contained herein.

SIMPLE....NOT EASY: A PRACTICAL GUIDE TO FINANCIAL HEALTH AND PROSPERITY

First edition. December 1, 2020.

Copyright © 2020 Jim Kilgore CFP®.

ISBN: 9798574968185

Written by Jim Kilgore CFP®.

Table of Contents

Introduction

"There are no shortcuts to any place worth going." Beverly Sills

For many years I have thought something needed doing about the lack of education people get during their formative years regarding the financial issues of life. Whether at home or in school, people don't come out of high school or college with the skills necessary to completely understand their finances. It is not until their financial mistakes add up, that they begin learning how to manage their finances well. My goal in writing this book is to help you live a financial life that is intentional. One that enables you to create the life you want, by setting goals, following a plan that brings those goals to reality, and sharing with you the habits that will make it all possible. Without a guide to help us, we humans tend to go with the flow; but with a plan, we can make active decisions that are intentional and put us one step closer to accomplishing what we set out to do.

We grow up, we graduate from high school, we might go to college or we go to work full time. Many of us will marry, have kids, and at some point, we'll have ten plates spinning at the same time. We have to figure out how to pay our student loan, pay for the kid's braces, pay the rent or mortgage, pay for school pictures, or cover the ordinary and necessary expenses we have in life and put a little in savings. Oh! and save for the kids' college fund and put away something for our retirement, all while dealing with *financial throat punches* along the way. **I define financial throat punches as unforeseen financial emergencies like a huge vet bill or car repair.**

All these things happening at the same time. With intention and planning, these financial issues are nothing more than a fly in your soup. None of it will happen by accident. Without a plan, you might accidentally spend too much on your vacation and charge more than you thought on your credit card. On a whim, you might buy a timeshare that will haunt you for the rest of your life. Knowing and understanding the types of financial decisions you will have to make and how to deal with them is the _key_ to personal financial success.

This is a book about building wise financial habits when you are young and building upon them year in and year out while making minor tweaks when necessary. What I want to do is provide you a roadmap that gives you the skills to achieve the personal and family financial goals you want to, no matter your timeline. As such, its topics include strategies to help you with goal setting to reach your financial goals, household budgeting, debt management, savings, and investing.

It is about the planning and execution of **smart financial decisions** all adults need to make at some point in their life. They don't teach this stuff in school when we're growing up, and even if they did, the research shows it wouldn't stick anyway. Do you remember the formula for finding the area of a trapezoid or how to graph a quadratic equation? Most things we learn, if we don't use them have a shelf life in our brains.

According to the National Center for Education Statistics, there are two forms of literacy the skills-based (operational) form of literacy which involves the use of printed materials such as reading, writing, and arithmetic. Then there is the task-based (conceptual) side of it. This form of literacy takes the first level and utilizes it in daily life. In other words, taking what you learn and using it to achieve your goals, and to develop your potential. Literacy involves more than just learning the general concepts but it's using them in your life for your benefit or the community in which you live.

My goal is to teach you more than just at the knowledge level of understanding but to take it a step further and get you to the point where you are applying the knowledge in your daily life to accomplish your personal financial goals. Ultimately, we all are given the same 24 hours each day. We don't know what tomorrow brings, but we do owe it to ourselves to be smart along the way, don't we? Who knows, you could get hit by a random tire flying through the window into the diner you like to eat at tomorrow morning, or you could just as easily be that person that lives to be 102 years old.

Having a plan for both of these situations is part of this book, so I hope you enjoy it. I intend it to be informative as well as entertaining so there'll be some satire sprinkled in along the way. Dad jokes only of course.

About The Author

"If there is one thing I know, it's my fantastic is talk" Andy Dwyer

My name is Jim, I grew up in a suburb of Dayton, Ohio in a town called West Carrollton. I didn't come from a wealthy family or one of status, but just a regular Midwestern home. We played outside as kids, played euchre at the dinner table, we went to the pool during the summer, had snowball fights in the winter, and, man, do we love our Marion's Pizza and Skyline Chili! I went to public school midway through the sixth grade until my parents saw the direction I was headed as an angry and temperamental kid from a broken home. They decided to send me to a Christian school, so midway through sixth grade, I went to Dayton Christian and that is where I graduated with a less than stellar GPA. I never intended on going to college when I graduated, but my parents were adamant about it, so I went to the local community college for a short stint to take auto mechanics classes.

I got my first job at 15-years-old, a paper route in the neighborhood. I wanted to start working earlier than that, but the lady that was in charge of the paperboys in the neighborhood said 15 was the earliest you could get a route. So, the day I turned 15, I got a paper route. Throughout my teenage years, I kept the paper route and mowed lawns with a high school friend of mine, and I always had money. Pretty soon I was working at the mall just to be near where the girls were hanging out. I always liked working for myself, which is odd because in 1995 I joined the Air Force. In the Air Force, you do what you are told, you follow orders, and you don't question authority. I spent 20 years in the Air Force and retired while stationed in South Dakota. I moved back home, got married, and got back into living in Ohio again.

One of the benefits of being in the Air Force was the time and money to go to school. I began taking college classes on base during lunch and in the evenings, and I eventually got my first Associate's Degree. During my 20 years in the Air Force, I amassed 230 semester hours of school and had no college debt. Finally, after three associate degrees, I decided on a major for my bachelor's degree: **Personal Financial Planning**.

When I retired from the Air Force in 2014, I began the journey to become a financial planner. I started with Northwestern Mutual for a short stint, but I didn't fit in there. Then I transferred to Raymond James, with an independent firm in Springboro, Ohio. After staying there for about two years I had an opportunity to join at a practice in Centerville, Ohio and I have been there since. We are fee-only and independent. This means we don't earn commissions on the products we sell, and we have a fiduciary duty to our clients. I am a Certified Financial Planning Professional as well as a Certified Financial Education Instructor and I have a passion for teaching people smart money habits they can use to thrive, not just survive in this life.

I truly love what I do, and I feel like I did back when I was a kid. I have the freedom to do what I want, and I don't feel like I have a "J.O.B." My hope in writing this book is that you will gain some insight into managing your finances in such a way that you achieve the goals you've set for yourself so that someday you will have the freedom to do whatever you want. For most people, they plan to save enough money to retire comfortably and relax and enjoy the sunset. For others, they are trying to save enough money so they can do what they want to do for the rest of their lives and not be tied down to a traditional job. The key is you get to define your *"why."*

My story is a story of major financial mistakes, because like most people I learned about money by doing something stupid. I don't want others to go through what I had to, to get their financial footing under them. For many of the people who read this book, I have lived what you are living. So, I feel I am especially qualified to talk about the issues in this book, not because of my education, or my credentials, but because I was at the bottom of the pit financially and clawed my way out.

Around 2003 I got a promotion in the Air Force which meant a significant raise in my monthly income. How did I celebrate? I went and got a couple more credit cards, bought a motorcycle, a car, and a house full of new stuff all on credit. Fast forward a few years and I was driving a beat-up pick-up truck, had a horrible credit score, constantly fought with my wife about money, and had creditors calling me every day for their money; all because I went and lost my mind for a short time with my finances. It took me several years to claw my way out of that pit and if I can help just one person not have to go through that, the effort I put into this book will be worth it.

I truly hope you enjoy the book and that you learn the concepts and incorporate them into your daily life. After all, isn't that what "education" is supposed to be about? Let me know what you think about my book by leaving a review.

What's the Point?

"The greatest enemy of excellence is good." Zig Ziglar

I didn't like school for many years. I hated school through high school and into college. The practical application of some of the stuff we had to learn growing up didn't make any sense to me and if you don't believe me ask my parents and they will tell you I did everything I could to fail out of school. My high school years were a seemingly never-ending cycle of mid-term grade reports, groundings, doing makeup work, getting report cards, more grounding. Despite all of that, I absorbed a lot of what they were trying to cram down my throat. The thing about education, in my humble opinion, is the current state of our education system is there are too many mandates and not enough hours in the day, so quality is pushed to the sideline and the amount of information is a mile wide and an inch deep.

As soon as a young person passes a standardized test, they dump that information and forget they ever learned it. Go ahead, think of something you know you learned in high school, that you don't use every day. Now, go graph inequality for me. You see, you probably had to google what that even was because you forgot it was a thing. I do want to add here, I know many hard-working, intelligent dedicated teachers and this is not an indictment on teachers. It is the system they work in, and they are not the culprit.

We learn all this stuff from kindergarten to 12th grade, and many of the things we need to learn, we don't. The practical items that plague our very existence on this planet go, for the most part, untaught. Think of how beneficial it would be to learn how dangerous advertising is and how many ads you will have flashed in front of your eyes every day? Think of how much more practical it would be for a young person to think about the kind of lifestyle they want to lead as an adult before they decide to go to college and get a degree in something that will saddle them with the equivalent of a mortgage payment before they get their first "real" job.

How about teaching kids how compound interest works against you just as much as it works for you and the snowball gets bigger in both directions if you don't control your spending. Concepts that once had to be drilled into our heads are just one internet search away. Critical thinking skills in all aspects of life have been shoved to the side and getting a passing score on a knowledge-based test has been the standard kids are now expected to live up to.

The list of things our young people have to "learn" to pass the test has gotten so long, that things like making change and teaching them to write in cursive have gone out the window. A young person goes to sign their drivers' license or write a check and **they print their name** because they have never had to learn to sign it. It looks like a third-grader writes their name. Ok, rant over and the reason for this book.

People need practical living skills that they will use to thrive in our society. Many employers and college campuses report 75% of young people <u>do not</u> have basic critical thinking and problem-solving skills. I am here to tell you, life is all about problem-solving. Many adults my age are not skilled at managing their household finances and make the same mistakes I did because these skills were not taught to them at school or home. Many older people I know never talked about money issues growing up and therefore, they muddled through life and learned by making the same mistakes many of us did.   For older generations too, money was a private matter and issues involving money were seldom discussed publicly. The effect this had, was that money was this mysterious thing and you were either good with it or you weren't.

My intention in writing this book is to bridge the gap between what you already know about money and help you thrive with your use of it. I am going to go through an intentional process to have you write down your goals as part of the journey you are going to take. To do that I will ask you to assess your *why*. The "why" you choose is a personal thing and will give you the drive and desire to stay on track when nothing else will. It will not be your goals, it will not be your monthly budget, it will be your *why* that makes you continue with this life-long process. After I help you define your *why* I am going to go through the most effective goal-setting process I have encountered to facilitate your goal setting in your own life. After you have your *why* and you've developed your goals, then we'll get into the nuts and bolts of the how. We will talk about debt, earning an income, creating a monthly budget to diligently save, and I will provide knowledge about investing your money. Then, I will go through taxes, insurance, and estate planning to protect it all, and wrap up with concluding thoughts, and finally, I will give you links to resources to help you on this journey.

When you are done reading this book, I want you to be able to go do what you have learned and apply it to your daily life to build strong habits that I did not build when I was young. Habits that will serve you well for the rest of your life, as you teach these habits to your children so they can teach them to their children, and so on.

I want to warn you though, you will be different than your friends. They might even think your financial discipline is weird. They will probably talk about you behind your back when you are not there. They will say things like, they are so cheap, or why don't they just get a new thingamabob as we did. You have got to decide what is more important; what they think or what you have that they don't….Psst hey, kid, it's more happiness and freedom. You see, when you live intentionally and follow the steps, I am about to layout for you in this book, you will have a life they never will because they did not plan for financial health and prosperity and you did.

Start with Goal Setting

"Success is the person who year after year reaches the highest limits in his field"   Sparky Anderson

What is a goal? Is it some abstract thought or idea that has no real meaning? Of course not, but a goal is just that….a goal. A goal is just a thought about what you would **like** to accomplish. Goals require a series of actions to accomplish, otherwise, it is a pipe dream. A long time ago I said to my younger self, "Jim someday you will run a marathon, if that person can do it, then you can too." Guess what? I still have not run a marathon, and I am not getting any younger. Do you know why I haven't run a marathon? Because running is horrible!!! Seriously, I never established a sincere desire to actually run a marathon and put together a running schedule to enable myself to accomplish it.

There is nothing special about making goals, just for the sake of setting one. As I said before, a goal without any action steps is just a pipe dream and stays that way until you put a plan in action. This book is a perfect example of a goal without any action steps. What I mean by that is I set the goal to have a book written over a year ago, and I even started pecking out some ideas in a word document. I kind of even wrote out the outline for the book at that time, but I never really sat down and intentionally went through the process I am about to share with you.

I gave myself a deadline, and that forced me to get the rest of my ideas down on paper, plan the chapters, and sit down and start writing. You see, if I hadn't finally drawn that line in the sand for myself, collected my thoughts, and moved forward, this book would still be a pipe dream.

Reaching financial independence, paying off debt, saving, and investing are all things that require action steps. I hear it all the time, oh I need to sit down and do some retirement planning, but I just don't have the time or many other excuses. The reality of it is that **people make time for the things that are important to them.**

I have friends that golf and they would not consider missing their weekly round of golf. They'll spend 4 hours on the golf course and a couple of hours in the clubhouse afterward and say they don't have time to talk about retirement, or life insurance, or estate planning. You see, they have not made these things a priority, so they get pushed to the back burner. If you are out there today and you have been saying to yourself, I want to get out of debt, or I want to get a handle on my household budget, so I can begin to save for retirement, what is getting in your way?

I am just as guilty of doing this over the years, so there is no judgment here. I was discussing with another business owner this week and they had no idea how their business had gotten so out of whack. They felt like any day they could be out of business. After talking for an hour or so, they realized it was because of their nearly instant success which had made them complacent. **They stopped doing the things they were doing at the beginning.** Making sure their clients were satisfied and following up with employees. Keeping open communication with their staff. All of those things slowly faded as their success bred laziness in their words.

What is the lesson here? You can be a victim of your success if you can reach your goals too quickly. It can cause you to take your eye off the ball. We have to continually challenge ourselves and add new goals and new challenges to what we want to achieve and put action steps in place to make those new goals achievable. As this pertains to financial goal setting, **reaching one financial goal can give you a false sense of security and if you are not careful, you'll slip back into old habits. I HAVE DONE IT!**

So let's talk about how all this goal-setting stuff pertains to the world of personal finance. This is not a magical process, but you have to be able to articulate what you want your goals to be. Examples of this might be some of the following.

- I want to retire at 60 and move to Florida on 60% of my current salary
- I want to travel to an exotic location for two weeks each year
- I want to ensure my children never have to worry about money
- I would like my business to pass to my children when I am ready to retire

You see these are very personal goals. Financial goals are not a one size fits all scenario. YOU get to decide what you want your financial goals to be. HERE IS THE KICKER, you have to follow the action steps that make achieving your goals possible. That is how goals are achieved.
I learned an acronym in the Air Force for proper goal setting.

They taught us that goals should be SMART.
Specific, **M**easurable, **A**ttainable, **R**elevant, and **Time-Bound**
Specific

For goals to work, you need to focus on exactly what you want to achieve. Your goal should be clear and specific, otherwise, you won't be able to focus your efforts or feel truly motivated to achieve it. Simply saying you want to be less stressed about money won't cut it. Be detailed, "I will pay off $20,000 in debt this year." When drafting your goal, try to answer the five "W" questions:

- **What** do I want to accomplish?
- **Why** is this goal important?
- **Who** is involved?
- **Where** is it located?
- **Which** resources or limits are involved?

Measurable

It's important to have measurable goals so that you can track your progress and stay motivated. Assessing progress helps you to stay focused, meet your deadlines, and feel the excitement of getting closer to achieving your goal. Give yourself daily, weekly, and/or monthly steps to help you see your progress. For example, you will have to pay $1,666.66 per month to reach your $20,000 goal.

A measurable goal should address questions such as:

- How much?
- How many?
- How will I know when it is accomplished?

Achievable

Your goal also needs to be realistic and attainable to be successful. In other words, it should stretch your abilities but remain possible. When you set an achievable goal, you may be able to identify previously overlooked opportunities or resources that can bring you closer to it.

An achievable goal will usually answer questions such as:

- How can I accomplish this goal?
- How realistic is the goal, based on other constraints

Relevant

This step is about ensuring that your goal matters to you and that it also aligns with other relevant goals. Trying to accomplish someone else's goal is the best way to fail. Just because your spouse or your Dad wants you to get out of debt, does not mean you'll want to. We all need support and assistance in achieving our goals, but it's important to retain control over them. So, make sure that your plans drive you forward, and that you're still responsible for achieving your own goal.

A relevant goal can answer "yes" to these questions:
- Does this seem worthwhile?
- Is this the right time?
- Does this match our other efforts/needs?

<u>Time-Bound</u>

Every goal needs a target date so that you have a deadline to focus on and something to work toward. This part of the SMART goal criteria helps to prevent everyday things from taking priority over your longer-term goals. Giving yourself a date for a goal gives you a target to aim at. It enables you to break things down per day, per week, per month to hit the target date for achieving your goal.

A time-bound goal will usually answer these questions:
- When?
- What can I do six months from now?
- What can I do six weeks from now?
- What can I do today?

SMART is an effective tool that provides the clarity, focus, and motivation you need to achieve your financial goals. It can also improve your ability to reach them by encouraging you to define your objectives and set a completion date. SMART goals are also easy to use by anyone, anywhere, in all aspects of your life. Bumps in the road will happen, that's ok. We live in a world where life happens, just stay focused and keep moving toward your goal using the <u>SMART</u> steps we have talked about here.

Steps to Setting Financial Goals

That is my goal-setting process, but how does all this pertain to **financial goal** setting? I am glad you asked. It is important at the beginning of this journey you understand where you are today. All journeys start with, you guessed it, your starting point.

Establish where you are by calculating your net worth. I have uploaded a simple net worth calculator you can download and use free of charge. Go to **www.thebuckeyefinanceguy.com** and it is available on the resources page. If you are lucky enough to be debt-free, you will most likely have a positive net worth. For some of you, you will start with a negative net worth because you have more debt(liabilities) than you have assets. Not to worry, this is the "where you are" part of the process. If you don't know where you are, you can't truly create a plan to get you where you want to go.

The next thing you will begin to do is formulate your financial goals by walking through the process I described. Use the **SMART** method I explained to identify your why. Creating your why is critical and you will lean on this throughout your journey. Once you have gone through the goal-setting process and you have your why, the financial goals you want to complete, then you will formulate the action steps to get you there.

These are going to be specific to your financial situation, so I can't give you what these will look like to you individually, but here are a couple of examples. An example might be to pay off all of my credit cards in the next 18 months. Another example might be, enroll in my company 401k plan and invest XX% of my income each month. Again, these are specific to what you are seeking to accomplish financially.

Finally, as with the goal-setting process you have to give yourself a timeline. People often muddle through life accidentally hitting some kind of financial comfort in life by working for 40 years and having a decent Social Security check by the time they retire. They might even manage to save $200,000 in the process in their company retirement plan.

The thing that is missing is the planning to set yourself up for a comfortable retirement. I think it is safe to say that you will not have a comfortable retirement if that is how you get there. Using the above example, pay off all of my credit card debt in the next 18 months has more power than just "pay off my credit card debt." You see, if you stop at pay off my credit cards, the procrastinator in you will come out. If you assign a timeline to the goal it is much more powerful. Sign up for my 401k by the end of this week and invest up to the company match. Now that is more specific and gives you a timeline.

Here is the secret to all of the financial mumbo jumbo you will ever see and here. You choose what your finances look like! Nobody else controls this. Facebook doesn't control it, the level of inflation does not control it, nor does the stock market, the financial pornography industry does not, nor the Federal Reserve. You and your behavior are the number one predictor of the outcomes you receive. Taking personal responsibility for setting your financial goals, following the action steps you give yourself, and staying the course will virtually guarantee you reach financial health and prosperity.

A Primer on Debt

"The rich rules over the poor, and the borrower is slave to the lender." Proverbs 22:7

Any personal finance book has to deal with the issue of debt in our society. So many people start their lives with great intention, and they get derailed like many of us. The temptation to buy things on credit that we don't need but we get sucked in because we've lived most of our lives in a get it now fast-food society. Americans are now drowning in debt; consumer debt in the US is roughly 14 trillion according to debt.org. Student loan debt is a large contributor to this as it approaches 1.6 trillion.

Within 6 months of graduation, the payments start on your student loans. With the average student loan debt hovering just north of $37,000 many new graduates are forced to move back in with parents as they struggle to meet the financial obligations of their student loan payments, rent, and their other living expenses. What used to mean a path to financial prosperity, has indeed changed. Many young people are headed to college to get degrees without understanding what their lifetime earnings potential will be with their chosen degree.

When they graduate, they are shocked at how high their payment is and many have no choice but to move back home with mom and dad. Couple that with the credit card companies sitting in the student union at the beginning of each school year offering credit cards like Halloween candy and you have the makings of a financial disaster.

Credit card debt has also hit critical mass in the U.S. Credit card debt crossed the trillion-dollar mark toward the end of 2019. More than 189 million Americans have credit cards, and the average credit cardholder has four cards. On average, each household with a credit card carries $8,398 in credit card debt.

If you are a young person and you are reading this book and to this point in your life you have managed to stay away from high-interest credit card debt or personal lines of credit, I highly recommend that you continue that habit. Sure, you will need to build credit somehow, but I would not suggest going out and getting a Visa card to do that.

One of the ways I have found to safely build your credit as a young person is to get a gas card either at one of the large chain gas stations across the country or one of the local ones that offer a low-interest credit card for gas purchases. Many times, you can get one of these cards it will have a low credit limit and you will only use the credit card to buy your gas for the month and pay it off completely at the end of the month before any interest charges are accrued.

Doing it like this you are removing the temptation to get that new shiny object that you've been wanting and putting it on a credit card. Having a card that you can only use for your monthly gas purchases keeps your self-discipline intact and will begin building your credit score. When I sat down to start writing my thoughts for this book I did not do so to take a deep dive into the issue of debt. I do think, however, as part of an overall personal finance book, the issue of debt simply has to be dealt with. There are plenty of books on the market that deal with getting yourself out of debt and so I don't want this chapter to be about that.

However, if you are reading this book and you are already in debt then I would use the following strategy to put you on the path to financial health. Before starting the debt pay-down plan that I'm going to layout for you, you must cut your monthly spending to the absolute bone to give yourself the maximum amount of discretionary income to put towards paying off your debt. Look through your bank statement for the last two or three months to find every single monthly charge that you forgot you're paying and eliminate that first. Then look at your other discretionary spending. Do you see a bunch of five-dollar coffees and lunches that you buy because you were too lazy to pack your lunch?

Make your coffee at home and pack your lunch every day and you will save on average nine dollars per day by doing this. Again, this book is as much about living an intentional life as is it is about personal finance. Packing your lunch is an intentional act that is giving you an extra margin in your monthly budget. Once you have gone through your bank statements and eliminated all of the unnecessary expenses in your life then you can start the bulleted list below.

- Make a list or create a spreadsheet of every one of your credit cards and debts.
- Rank them from the highest interest rate to the lowest
- Pay the minimum payment on every card except for the one with the highest interest rate
- Put every extra dollar you can put towards the credit card with the largest interest rate every month until it's paid off
- Once that card is paid off move to the next card by taking the money that you were putting towards the first card adding to it the minimum payment on the second card and do this until it is paid off
- Follow this process until you have every single one of your high-interest credit cards paid in full and never use them again.
- If one of these debts includes a student loan, pay it off in the same manner as you would any other high-interest credit card

If you are interested, you can go to my website at **www.thebuckeyefinanceguy.com** and download a spreadsheet that I created to help you with your *debt pay-down strategy.*

After you have a handle on your debt and the elimination of it from a high-interest revolving credit standpoint, you can deal with any other outstanding debts that you have. I am not a diehard don't have any debt kind of financial planner or financial coach. If you don't have a car payment in addition to a bunch of other debts, you will have more discretionary income to put towards your savings and investing goals. I am also somewhat of a realist and understand that a reliable car that can get you to and from your job that enables you to save and invest is an important tool in your toolbox.

A car smartly purchased with a low-interest rate and a warranty removes any doubt about getting you to and from work every day, so you can meet the financial goals you have established. I wouldn't suggest going out and getting a 2020 Ford Mustang Selene, and exclaiming you needed reliable transportation. Come on, that would be dumb, nobody would do that, right? Your level of debt is the dangerous part, and understanding it is what is holding the majority of people back from financial freedom is the point. The elimination of that debt frees you up to do so many other things with your money.

Ok, so you have managed to get yourself into a position of financial health by paying off your credit cards and keeping your car payment reasonable because you opted for the Hyundai instead of the Mustang. You are ready to look at buying a home. What I believe is the best way to identify and purchase a home and keep you ahead when it comes to building your financial independence. It is called the 30/30/3 home-buying rule. First, you have to understand how realtors and mortgage lenders get paid.

Buying a Home

      Something I highly encourage people to consider when they decide to purchase a home is how much home is enough, as opposed to how much home they can afford. Homes are sold through realtors and mortgages are obtained through banks and mortgage brokers. Realtors make a commission on the sale as a fixed percentage of the home value. The industry standard is around 6% and the realtor gets to keep the whole thing if they list and sell your home, minus the fee paid to their broker. If there are two realtors involved, one that lists is not the one the finds the buyer, the two realtors split the 6% and give their broker their portion of their commission. On the mortgage side of things, the mortgage broker gets an origination fee on the mortgage and some other fees. The origination fee is a percentage of the mortgage value, so bigger mortgage, bigger paycheck. Can you see how the bigger the home you buy, and finance is good for the realtor and mortgage broker and not necessarily in your best interest? Obviously, there are some great real estate agents and mortgage brokers out there that do right by their clients, but there are also a lot of scumbags out there too.

      It is smart to have a general idea of a couple of things when you decide to buy a home. First, how much home you need, and the following three guidelines I am going to share with you. Setting some parameters to follow will keep you from buying too much house and potentially putting yourself in a compromising position down the road if you get laid off, or some other event that causes you financial hardship.

First, decide how much home is enough and stick to it. If you are newly married and you plan on having a couple of kids, then perhaps a three-bedroom house with a couple of baths is enough. Do not, I repeat do not get caught up in the "interest rates are so low we can afford more house fiasco." Getting sucked into that is a recipe for financial ruin. Decide how much is enough house and find one that fits those parameters. You are going to have to use some judgement here and so this is just the start of the home buying process.

The following three guidelines will help shape this decision as well.

Number 1: Spend no more than 30% of your gross income on a monthly mortgage.

Industry standards pretty much say 30% of your gross income on your mortgage is the maximum you should spend on your mortgage payment. As mortgage rates decline people are tempted to increase the percentage. When you get a lower rate, you can buy more home if you keep your spending as a percentage of gross income fixed. The sirens go off when you break this rule and stretch beyond the 30% mark. The people most at risk of breaking this rule are the middle to lower-income folks.

You simply have to be able to take care of your basic needs with the remaining money so spending less of your monthly gross on your mortgage will give you the peace of mind knowing your other needs can be met. I recommend your all-in mortgage payment not exceed 30% of your monthly gross take home pay. That means if you don't put down 20% and you opt for a lower down payment and have to pay Private Mortgage Insurance (PMI), then 30% is still your cap on all in mortgage payment. All in will include principle, interest, property tax, homeowner's insurance, and PMI.

Number 2: Use leverage to your advantage

Leverage is defined as using someone else's money to your advantage or the use of it to control a greater amount of assets by borrowing money to increase your return. At least in the investment world that is the definition. Leveraging the use and enjoyment of your home and using someone else's money to do it is just smart. Think about it, right now you can borrow money for **30 years** at 2.75% and you can use very little of your own personal capital to do it.

Your home shelters you, it can appreciate (typically 3.9% per year) in value all while you are paying down the mortgage (FHFA.gov). The 3.9% appreciation in your home value is an inflation hedge and is the foundation of the process of building wealth. U.S inflation averages 3.2% per year according to usinflationdata.com (2020). Many people I know have folded their starter home into their next home, and then into their next home by capitalizing on this price appreciation during housing market booms. Additionally, you get to use and enjoy your home, raise your kids, have friends over for dinner, and live the American dream.

If you go to fhfa.gov, they have a home price inflation calculator that can show you the home price appreciation for houses in your area. It is a pretty handy tool, and it can give you an idea of what your home could be worth today. I took a couple of random dates and put them in the calculator, so your results might vary, but for the area of the country I live in, these were the results. If you purchased a home in the Cincinnati Ohio region in the $330,000 range in May of 2016, the estimated home value on November 2, 2020, is $424,000. That is nearly a $100,000 price increase in 4 ½ years. These are not typical results, but hopefully, you can see some of the power of homeownership and how it can be a great creator of wealth if you make wise decisions.

Are you starting to see how wise decisions start adding up to the positive, and how dumb decisions work against you? The essence of financial health and prosperity is making more wise decisions than stupid ones as it pertains to your personal finances.

Number 3: Limit the value of your home purchase to no more than 3x your annual gross household income.

Affording your home based on cash flow is a function of the price you pay for your home. If you follow the first two rules, then you can tie all of this together with this rule. This rule is a super quick way to filter homes in your price range. This rule takes into account the down payment percentages and prevents you from stretching too far.

For example, if you earn $100,000 in combined gross income with your spouse, you can comfortably afford a home that is up to $300,000. To reiterate, with mortgage rates dropping, housing affordability has gone up. It can be tempting to try to stretch this to 5x your income, but just know if you do that you will have higher property taxes, insurance, maintenance, and household expenses to go with it. BIG HOUSE, BIG BILLS.

I am a homeowner, and I understand your desire to own a nice home. We want to live the fullest life we can, and it is hard to wait when we have been so conditioned to get it now in our fast-food society. Despite all of these advantages, do not be tempted to overextend your finances when buying a home. When you buy more home than you need, all the other expenses go up with it. You will have higher property tax, utility payments, and maintenance costs just to name a few. The stress will take a toll on you and you will realize it was not worth it. At the very least, follow this rule when buying a home. It will be good for you in the long run and save you from learning some tough financial lessons the hard way.

Your Income

"Success is not so much what we have as it is what we are." Jim
Rohn

When I give presentations I often ask, what is your
most valuable asset? 100% of the time someone yells out
"your house" and 100% of the time they are wrong. Your
most valuable asset is your ability to earn a living. If you are a
young person reading this book, remember I said nobody gets
to choose for you what your life will look like. The choices
you make determine that. As much as any other choice, your
career choice will determine your lifetime earning potential.

Parents, I encourage you to have discussions with your
children about the career choices they are looking at making.
You need to promote critical thinking here. If they want to
study the mating habits of exotic birds, they need to
understand there is going to be a limited market for that
particular choice. Again, if that is the path they take, they
make the choice and determine their financial outcomes and
lifetime earnings potential. As long as they understand that,
and it meets with the kind of lifestyle they want to lead, then
great, more power to them.

However, if that is the profession they choose, you
have to get them to understand they will not have the same
lifestyle as a professional business executive. The disconnect
between job choice and lifestyle is one that is staring us in the
face. We have many young people right now that have grown
up in a solid upper-middle-class home headed to college to
get a degree is some basic non-sense and they graduate and
think they are entitled to the same lifestyle they had growing
up. They fail to realize their parents made different choices
than they did and have worked many years to reach their
level of income and success. Of course, part of this comes
from our get it now society, but the other part comes from a
failure to set expectations, to begin with.

To solidify the concept, I want to go through a couple of examples. I am going to start by going through an example of a married couple who are both brand new college graduates and they both just got their first full-time jobs. Now, this couple didn't spend any time mapping out what they hoped to accomplish with their degrees, they just went to college because that is what society expects of young people….right!?

John got a degree in adventure education because he loves the outdoors and thought it'd make a great career. Starting his first year, he makes $21,854. His wife Jane was on the golf team throughout high school and college and she got a partial scholarship. She went to college and got her degree in turfgrass science. The way she saw it, she wanted to be around golf, because she enjoys it so much. Her first-year salary is $35,340. He completely financed his degree, and she got a partial scholarship as I mentioned previously.

Combined they have $72,000 in student loan debt with an 8% interest rate. With annual raises and cost of living increases, they have a lifetime earnings potential of $4,889,165. Wow, that is a huge number!! Not so fast, look at the next example with a couple that both took an active role in picking their degree and why.

Bill went to college and got a degree in accounting because when he was researching careers that would be in demand, accounting was always near the top. He got his first accounting job out of college at the low end of the scale because he is still studying for the CPA exam, his starting salary is $49,682. Marcy, his wife went to school for architectural design. Again, she wanted to do something she felt she would enjoy, but at the same time wanted something that would be in demand. She interned in college for a small firm and they hired her after graduation, so she got a little higher pay because they knew the kind of work ethic she had. Combined, their lifetime earnings estimate with the cost of living/annual raises is $8,801,079. Bill and Marcy both applied for a bunch of scholarships when they went to school and after their first year were awarded large scholarships and have little to no college debt.

Above, we have two very different scenarios with two drastically different lifetime earnings outcomes. Now, both can do very well if they make wise financial decisions along the way. Both of their problems are that they have not read this book, so who knows what will happen. In all seriousness, the couple that made some intentional decisions is in a way better position than the couple just kind of winging it.

We have some serious decisions to make about what we do with our money and how we spend it knowing there is a finite number out there that we can make in our lifetimes. It pays to have a plan for what you are going to do with your money. As many of us already know, life happens fast, and making smart decisions can set you up for success. The opposite is also true.

Now, which one of these couples do you think is more likely to sit down and make some intentional decisions regarding their finances? Probably the couple that showed some planning concerning their education, but that does not mean that John and Jane are screwed, but it does mean they need to make some plans quickly or they have the potential of getting caught up in more whimsy.

Both of these couples still get to choose the kind of lifestyle they want to live, and they can both end up with some very nice assets down the road if they properly allocate their resources. If they skip the part about staying out of debt because they get caught up in the "keep up with the Joneses" mentality many people do, take on too much revolving debt, or they buy more house they can afford, they both stand a chance of handcuffing their financial health and prosperity. Don't miss this very important point, both of these couples had control over where they went to college, what they studied, and how they paid for it. It was the way the decision-making process differed that set them apart and made one have a higher lifetime earnings percentage than the other. Now that we have an idea of how our lifetime income potential affects our lifestyle, let's take a look at budgeting to reach financial health and prosperity.

I want to be clear on this, I do not believe in the college for all mentality. College is not for everyone, nor does it guarantee success. Putting thought into your career choice is the point here. There are many career choices out there that have great pay without the need for college. Many two-year programs pay very well, and the trades are suffering from a lack of new entrants into them. A plumber, electrician, or heating ventilation and air conditioning tradesperson can make a significant salary. Many of them I know can work as many hours as they want because the demand is so high, and the pay is incredible.

I know a couple of people that I am proud to call clients. They have worked hard their entire life and their earnings have been fairly average for the last 40 years. One of them worked their way up through a local landscaping company to the position of management and makes about $35,000 per year and her husband, is the landscape foreman for another company. Combined they have made a pretty typical middle-class income for their entire working life. They have diligently saved and have nearly a million dollars in retirement savings to accompany their nice social security benefit. They are now in their mid-sixties and have enough saved to maintain the same lifestyle for the rest of their lives. Neither one of them has a college degree, and they have both determined to work hard, save diligently, and live within their means.

Budgeting to Reach Your Goals

"You don't get in life what you want; you get in life what you are."
Les Brown

I have had people tell me that budgets are antiquated and a thing of the past. Now, these are the same people spending $5.00 per day at a fancy coffee shop and nothing saved for retirement, but sure budgets are a thing of the past. Alright, rant over. Creating a budget, and following every month has several beneficial effects.   First, you are telling your money where to go, rather than wondering where it went. Second, you can assign a portion of your take-home each month to savings and investing.

PUBLIC SERVICE ANNOUNCEMENT: You don't have to spend every dime you earn each month. I talk to hundreds of people per year and I always ask them if they live on a budget. Darn it if the most successful people I know, people who have plenty of savings and investments, all say they do have a monthly budget. Conversely, the people I run into that are always broke and live paycheck to paycheck, don't. I will tell you, creating and living on a budget WILL change your financial life for the better. There are a ton of different ways you can budget. You can use a pen and paper and write it out, a spreadsheet, an app on your phone, envelopes, or anything that works for you.

I prefer a spreadsheet with formulas that add and subtract everything for me. If you'd like, you can go to the resources page on my website at **www.thebuckeyefinanceguy.com** and download my budgeting form to help you do a budget every month. Budgeting is about your household cashflow management. If you own a business, the success or failure of your business comes down to positive cash flow. A monthly budget will help you create positive cash flow at the household level. By filling out your budget each month, your financial plan will begin to reveal itself right before your eyes. You will see problem areas and learn how to close the valve of needless spending because you will know where every dollar is going.

Be warned, it will take you a while to complete your budget for the first time. This is new, and new things are not as easy to do as things you've done for a while. Remember learning to tie your shoes? I do, and I know my dad was about to kill me because I just couldn't get it. After tying my shoes for a while, I could do it with my eyes shut. I assure you, the more you do this, the easier it gets.

The process is going to look like this. At the end of each month, let's call it the very last day of the month for ease. You and your spouse will sit down together and do the budget for the upcoming month. For instance, on 30 September you will sit down together at the dinner table and go through your incomes for October and you will assign every single dollar of your income a place to go. It can go to groceries or electricity, or you can set a portion aside for eating dinner out a couple of times per month.

The key is that every dollar is allocated to something on this sheet (some of it can and should be to savings/investing). On 31 October, you complete the spent column from the budget you completed on 30 September. Then, you move forward with the November budget and assign every dollar a place to go. After a few months, you will have made some adjustments to the budgeted/spent columns as you zero in on your monthly averages.

If you have debts you are paying off, you are going to include each one of those based on the debt pay down section. If you need to go back and review, please do so. I have all of the spreadsheets on my website for your use to assist you in this journey. Each one of the resources has some instructions on how to complete them. It isn't rocket science, but it can be confusing at first. If you have difficulty with completing the forms, send me an email at **jim.kilgore@thebuckeyefinanceguy.com,** and will be delighted to help.

Some magic is going to start happening when you and your spouse sit down each month and complete your budget. First, marital communication and understanding will happen. You will start having discussions about money, and you will most likely start fighting less about it. Many divorcing/divorced couples site fights about finances as the number one cause of divorce.

Next, you will catch yourself saying things like, "That's not in the budget." Your spending and saving activity will become intentional and your blossoming financial health will begin to become clear to you. You will begin to see your goals come to fruition and this will give you increased resolve to keep up the work. As time goes by your debts will go down and your net worth will go up. You and your family will begin to see financial health and prosperity bloom right before your eyes.

I hope this section has been eye-opening. I know crafting and living on a budget works because I have seen the results in so many family's lives, I can't count. Follow the process and do it for six months, and I can almost guarantee a drastic change in your family finances. Now that you have a handle on your household cash flow, it is time to talk about saving for the short term as well as the long term.

Saving & Investing

"The price of excellence is discipline. The cost of mediocrity is disappointment."   *William A. Ward*

If you are paying off debt during this process of budgeting and saving, it is important to have a cash buffer in savings in case of an emergency and you need to pay for a car repair, a home repair, or some other kind of unforeseen event in your life. You should attempt to have a $1,000 emergency fund in your savings account only and I repeat only for household emergencies.

Once you have your emergency fund, and you are six months into living on your budget. It is time to calculate your average monthly ordinary and necessary expenses. I define ordinary and necessary as rent or mortgage, all utilities (electric, water, gas), food, and all car expenses. Then, you are going to put 6 months of living expenses in liquid savings. That way if you lose your job, you have six months of living expenses saved while you look for a new one. If you get unemployment benefits, it will help stretch your savings to 7 to 8 months. You say "What about Netflix, my cell phone, and cable. I say those are not necessary, but if you want to add those to the total, go right ahead.

After you have your six months of living expenses saved, then you can get serious about investing in your financial independence. Financial independence is defined however you want to define it. That can be retirement at some later date, like 65. Although, financial independence can also mean having enough money, so you don't have to have a traditional job. Maybe you want to start your own business, travel the world starting at age 50, or any other goal you set for yourself. Putting enough money in investments and growing them for many years is what the next section is about.

Risk

No section on investing would be complete without talking about *risk*. Understanding the risks of the types of investments you are in is the first step in investing. I am going to go through the most common types of risks and their definitions first and I will focus just on stocks and bonds when it comes to growing your nest egg. Investing, in general, involves risk, but thoughtful investing that keeps your goals as well as the risks of your investments, keep the overall risk at an acceptable level. Risk is defined as the degree of uncertainty and/or the potential of loss inherent in an investment.

Every saving and investing product have different risks and returns. These differences include how readily investors can get their money when they need it, how fast their money will grow, and how safe their money will be. In this section, I will go through the following types of risks: business risk, volatility risk, inflation risk, liquidity risk, systematic and unsystematic risk. I will also address fees as well as building a diversified portfolio.

Business Risk

When you buy a stock, you are purchasing a piece of that business and you are one of its owners as a shareholder. With a bond, you are loaning the company money and are considered a lender. Returns from each of these scenarios require the company to stay in business. If a company goes belly up, assets are liquidated, common shareholders are the last in line in the proceeds of the sale. Bondholders are paid ahead of common and preferred shareholders. Business risk involves the risk in that particular company rather than the market as a whole.

Volatility Risk

Even when companies are doing great, their share prices can fluctuate up and down quite a bit. Large company stocks on average have lost money as a group on average one out of every three years. Market fluctuation can be unnerving for some investors. A stock price can be affected by many things and with the financial media on 24 hours per day, 7 days a week, 365 days a year, they are always trying to throw a monkey wrench into things. Politics, market events, worldwide disasters can all affect the market in the short term.

I do want to note, the only losses you suffer during a down year are ones *you* lock in by selling when the market is down. Market losses are always paper losses until *you* sell and make them permanent. Keeping your cool through the ups and downs in the market is the key to investing success. If you can't sit tight through a 10% decline once a year on average, you need to assess your ability to do this on your own and hire a professional to do it for you.

Inflation Risk

Inflation is the general upward movement of the price of things. Inflation reduces purchasing power, which is a risk for investors receiving a fixed rate of interest. The principal concern for individuals investing in cash or cash equivalent investments is that inflation will erode their purchasing power over time.

Interest Rate Risk

Interest rate changes can affect the value of a bond. If bonds are held to maturity the investor will receive back the face value, plus the interest. If sold before maturity, the bond may be worth more or less than the face value. Rising interest rates will make newly issued bonds more attractive to investors because newer bonds have a higher rate of interest than older ones. To sell an older bond with a lower interest rate, you might (probably will) have to sell it at a discount.

Liquidity Risk

Liquidity risk refers to the risk that an investor won't find a market for their securities, potentially preventing them from buying or selling when they want to. This can be the case with more complicated, thinly traded securities. Thinly traded securities are defined as not having any significant daily trading volume. It may also be the case with investments that charge a penalty for early withdrawal or liquidation, such as a certificate of deposit (CD).

Systematic Risk

Systematic risk refers to the risk inherent to the overall market. Systematic risk is also known as undiversifiable risk because this type of risk affects the entire market, not just a particular stock or segment. When the coronavirus pandemic hit the market in early 2020, the stock market plummeted for a month before getting its feet back under it. Almost every segment of the market was affected and no amount of diversification in stocks kept you from at least a partial decline. If you were lucky enough to have a professional advisor managing your money, you may have been down less, but you were still down.

Unsystematic Risk

Unsystematic risk refers to the risk inherent in a specific company or industry. By investing in a range of companies and different industries, unsystematic risk can be drastically reduced through diversification.

Fees

When it comes to the topic of fees when you are investing you want to keep them as low as possible. If investing your savings is something you are comfortable doing, then by all means do it. Most people do not have the temperament to ride out the violent swings in the market without making an emotional decision to sell at the wrong time. That is not to say you can't do it yourself, but the best thing to do in this situation is not to watch the financial pornography available 24/7.

If you are going to go it alone, I'd recommend looking at your portfolio as little as possible and set up an automatic process where you are investing on a weekly/monthly basis and you have an automatic investing system set up where you are buying set amounts of each investment through the ups and downs of the market. Seldom look at your statement and you should have a lifetime return higher than that of all your friends and neighbors. If you can't do that or you think you will be tempted to tweak things, or heaven forbid sell out when the market goes down 10%, then hire a professional to manage your investments.

A few more words about this to drive this point home. Stocks represent the ownership of businesses. I don't believe anyone can be a successful investor without seeing that. Mainstream companies are generally rational, profit-seeking businesses, run by highly compensated professionals for the benefit of their shareholders. That person's job is to enhance shareholder value over time.

For over a century, stocks have provided compound returns exceeding three times the general rate of inflation. They have been the greatest generator of real wealth available to common people. I believe, as many others do, they will continue to do so.

Stocks do go through ups and downs. If you can't ride out a solid double-digit correction every year, and the reduction of your capital by an average of one third one year in five, you simply can't be an equity investor. Temporary declines in a well-diversified equity portfolio are as common as a cold. Over a lifetime of investing, they are of different depths and durations, but they are just blips. Permanent loss in a portfolio is always caused by human emotional error, not by the market.

So, I say it again, if you can't ride out the ups and downs of the market over the long haul, then hire a professional to do it. An advisor will most likely charge a fee based on a percentage of the assets they manage. A very common range for this is between 1-1.5% depending on the size of your account and can be lower than that, but do you want the lowest bidder if you are going to hire a professional?

The advisor will more than make up for the fee they charge by keeping you from permanent loss in your portfolio if you were managing it alone and decided to sell at the wrong time. If you do decide to go it alone, you are going to want to look at investments with very low management fees.

There are thousands of mutual funds, exchange-traded funds (ETF's), and all of them have fees. Some of them are very low. ETFs have some of the lowest fees and have a professional managing the investments for you. You can find some very low-cost ETFs and mutual funds that give you the diversification you need in small, medium, and large companies in different sectors of the economy and around the globe. Vanguard is known for its very low-cost funds in a variety of different flavors. You can build a nicely diversified portfolio of stock and bond ETF's using Vanguard for example.

To show you how fees affect the lifetime investment return, I am going to give you an example. Understand, this is a very simplistic calculation, but I want to show you the difference between a fund that would be considered a high fee, versus one that would be considered low. Let's say you invested $10,000 today in a fund with a 1% annual fee and you let it grow for 35 years and never added another dime. With an average annual return of 7% from your fund at the end of 35 years your investment would be worth $75,104. Now take those same parameters and reduce the fee to .03 and let's see what happens. With the low fee after 35 years, your investment would be $105,650. The difference in those two numbers, just by keeping fees low is 40.67%. That is astonishing and why taking care to monitor your fees is so important.

Another alternative is to buy individual stocks in companies you feel are strong and will provide you with the shareholder return you are looking for. I might think about saving for a few years in a low-cost ETF portfolio before I jumped in and bought stocks, otherwise, you may find you have a very concentrated portfolio for a long period while you save and buy more companies. Buying individual stocks doesn't have any fees outside of the trading fee's you'll pay to buy or sell the stocks. This strategy takes much more effort and maintenance than buying funds with professional managers or paying an investment advisor to do it for you.

Take for example General Electric. If you bought General Electric and decided to just hold onto it without following its financials and the health of the company, then you would have gotten burned. At one time, GE was one of the most profitable, most well run companies in the country. That could not be said of GE today. Buying individual stocks is going to necessitate you tracking the companies you own to ensure they stay profitable and offer you the shareholder value you need to grow your portfolio.

Building a Diversified Portfolio

Ok, so we have talked about the risks of investing in this chapter, and I have gone over how important fees are to your long-term growth. Now, let's get into what a diversified portfolio of ETFs would look like. This is an example portfolio and not a real portfolio that I or anyone else I know has or uses, so trying to duplicate this, you do so at your own risk, and I take no responsibility for the success or failure of this portfolio.

You will want to decide how many funds you want to have because some of the share prices can be kind of high, you might start with just a couple of funds, and as your portfolio grows, spread some of the risks out among different areas. You might start with the Vanguard S&P 500 ETF (VOO). This fund strives to match the return of the S&P 500 and owns a basket of stocks that mimic the actual index. Its expense ratio is .035 so it meets the low fees you are looking for. The S&P 500 includes roughly that many companies, representing 500 of the strongest, most well run companies in the U.S. and the world. If one company falters, you have the other roughly 499 to make up for that one. Next, you might think about adding QQQE this fund is called Nasdaq 100 Equal Weighted Index. It strives to match the Nasdaq 100 Equal Weighted Index and the fund includes approximately 100 of the largest domestic non-financial companies listed on the Nasdaq. It has low fees as well at .35%. Another option is the ProShares S&P 500 Dividend Aristocrats ETF (NOBL). To be a Dividend Aristocrat a company has to have paid and increased its dividend for 25 consecutive years. This fund also has a very low expense ratio at .35%. You might round this portfolio out by adding an emerging markets ETF as well as a bond fund to have that asset class in the mix.

The above example would give you adequate diversification and if you set up a monthly investment program into those funds and reinvested dividends for many years, you would end up with a nice sized investment account when it is all said and done.

In this chapter, we went over risk, the importance of managing your fees, and how to build a diversified portfolio. Now let's shift the discussion to that of protecting you and your family in case something bad happens along the way.

Insurance

"If there is a better way to do it...find it." Thomas A. Edison

Typically, I encourage the proper allocation of the family budget to insurance coverage before investing, because my belief is outside of the financial plan itself, **insurance is the foundation of wise planning**. However, since I wanted you to actually read my book and not throw it away, I put it here in the hope that I have gotten you sufficiently interested to continue reading.

Life insurance. Almost nobody wants to talk about life insurance, because it makes them think about their death. Understandably then life insurance is often *sold not bought*. What I mean by that, is very few people wake up in the morning and say to themselves "You know what, I want to get some life insurance quotes today." More likely, they are introduced to a life insurance agent or are approached by a member of the family that sells life insurance, and the process begins.

There are many names for life insurance policies, but only two kinds. The two kinds are **term and permanent**. We are going to walk through the different kinds of term and permanent life insurance policies and explain some of the different features of each. This is going to be an overview and we are not going to endorse any particular insurance carrier, but just describe some of the most often seen policy designs in the process, to give you a deeper understanding of these products, and how they lay the foundation of your financial plan.

<u>**Term Life Insurance.**</u>

Term life insurance lasts for a set number of years before it expires. If you die before the term is up, a set amount of money, known as the death benefit, is paid to your designated beneficiary. Term life insurance is considered the simplest, and most accessible life insurance policy for most people. When you make your payments (known as your premium), you're simply paying for the death benefit that goes to your beneficiaries in the event of your death. The death benefit can be paid out as a lump sum, a monthly payment, or an annuity. Most people elect to receive their death benefit as a lump sum.

Term life insurance policies are more affordable than other types of life insurance policies, usually costing between $30-40 a month for a 30-year, $500,000 policy for healthy people in their 20s and 30s. They expire at the end of the term, which can last up to 35 years.

Depending on the type of term life insurance you have, the premiums can: stay the same for the length of the policy, increase over time, or in rare cases decrease over time.
The purpose of life insurance is to protect your loved ones from financial obligations if you're not around to provide for them. When you're still saving for retirement, paying off a mortgage, or raising children and planning on sending them to college, life insurance makes sense. But eventually, you'll have saved for retirement through a 401(k) or IRA, you'll have paid off your mortgage, and your kids will be out of the house with families of their own.

The fact that term life insurance expires, and there are no additional fees associated with it, is what makes it the most affordable life insurance option. Don't fret that your life insurance policy expires **that could be part of your financial plan**.

You have several options if your term expires. First, you can purchase a new term policy, but understand the premium will likely be somewhat higher. Some policies allow you to convert to permanent life insurance, or some allow a return of premium. Meaning, if you bought a term policy with a return of premium rider, if you lived through the term, you would get all your money back.

So those are the basics of term life insurance, there are many different policy options, so if you need some term life insurance contact an agent you know and trust or I would be happy to discuss your options with you. Now on to the permanent insurance products.

Whole Life

Whole life insurance, on the other hand, is considered a permanent life insurance policy because it does not expire. It has a death benefit but also a cash value, which is a tax-deferred savings account that is included in the policy. The cash value accrues interest at a predetermined fixed rate. Each month, a certain portion of your premium will go into the cash value of the policy, which offers a guaranteed rate of return (The exact amount that goes into savings is determined by your policy). The policy's cash value grows over time. Due to the fees and the extra features, a whole life insurance policy can cost five to fifteen times as much as a term life policy (for the same death benefit amount).

Whole life lasts for as long as you pay the premiums. However, the cash value component can make whole life more complex than term life because you have to consider surrender fees, taxes, and interest as well as other stipulations. Still, it may be worth it if you need the cash value to cover things like endowments or estate taxes, which might benefit from the options that a whole life policy provides.

<u>**Universal life insurance**</u>

Universal life also has a cash value, just like a traditional whole life insurance policy. Your premiums go toward both the cash value and the death benefit. But there's a twist: the policyholders of universal life policies can change the premium and death benefit amounts without getting a new policy. Although you have a minimum premium to keep the policy in force, you can use the cash value to pay the premium. That means if you have enough money in the cash value, you can use that to skip premium payments entirely, letting the accrued interest do the work. But the cash value of a universal life insurance policy has an interest rate that's sensitive to current market interest rates. If the interest rate is credited to your policy decreases to the minimum rate, your premium would have to increase to offset the reduced cash value.

This flexibility makes universal life insurance attractive to some people, but it's also confusing. Unlike term life insurance, where you pay a certain amount every month or year and know what the death benefit will be, shifting premiums and death benefits are more complex than what most people need, and it comes at an added cost.

Variable life insurance

Variable life is similar to whole life insurance in that they both have a cash value, but the functions of the cash values are quite different. With a whole life insurance policy, the cash value component is a savings account. That's why, although the growth might be small compared to other investment options, there is a guaranteed minimum rate. It also includes dividend payments from the life insurance company. A variable life insurance cash value, though, is more akin to investing. The money paid into it goes into a series of mutual fund-like sub-accounts where you can get some decent growth, but you can also lose money depending on the market. The cash value is more or less placed in the stock market.

Variable Universal Life

If you think variable universal life insurance is just some aspects of universal and variable life insurance policies mashed together…well, you're mostly right.
A variable universal life insurance policy takes the best (or worst, depending on how you look at it) of the other two policies: you can adjust the premium and death benefit amount while investing the cash value in the policy's sub-accounts. But variable universal life insurance also comes with many of the same elements as the other two. Again, this policy is more complicated than most people need, and it isn't your best investment or insurance option.
There are other flavors of life insurance out there, but this pretty much covers the main ones, and I certainly don't want to bore you to death.

In my humble opinion, trying to mix an insurance product with investments is silly. Keep your insurance costs low and diversify your investments the way I explained in the previous chapter. It is rare when I come across someone who needs a whole life (permanent) insurance policy, so for most people a 30- or 35-year level term policy to cover their working years is more than adequate. Most insurance policies require some type of medical testing to qualify, but some do not. Each insurance carrier has their underwriting standards.

Disability Insurance

Disability insurance is often overlooked because when you are young and healthy, you have a hard time seeing that you could ever get hurt and miss work, let alone for a few months. The statistics on the chances of you having a short-term disability some time in your life are pretty eye-opening. A 35-year-old has a 50% chance of becoming disabled for 90 days or longer before age 65. About 30% of Americans ages 35-65 will suffer a disability lasting longer than 90 days during their working careers. More than 375,000 people become completely disabled every year in the U.S. (U.S. Department of Labor Statistics). Nearly half of all foreclosures (46%) on conventional mortgages are due to disability. It has been estimated that disability causes foreclosure 16 times more often than death does (Lifeinsure.com).

With these statistics in mind, let me walk through how disability insurance works. If you have short term disability through your work and you become injured **at work**, then you will most likely be covered by workers compensation. If a non-job-related issue comes up, your employer-provided short-term disability coverage will likely cover you. However, many of the short-term disability policies only cover up to 60% of your monthly take-home, so there will be a gap in your monthly income if this occurs.

This is where having your emergency fund and your 3-6 months of living expenses comes in. If or when you have a short-term disability, your 3-6 months of expenses will last you much longer because you are still getting at least a percentage of your monthly income from your disability policy. I was contemplating shortening short term disability to STD but realized that might confuse people, so I decided not to. Back to the task at hand. Each short-term disability policy is different, so you must understand yours. It might not kick in for 30 days, and only cover up to a 90-day disability. These are the kinds of provisions you need to understand about your employee benefits plan, so you can plan your finances accordingly.

Long term disability coverage is a different beast. Plans can be expensive but understanding how this works, will give you the information you need to make an informed decision about whether you think you need one. With long-term disability policies, there are a few definitions we need to address. First, is "own occupation" or "any occupation." Any occupation means you can file a claim if you are permanently disabled and cannot work in any occupation you are suited to by education, training, or experience. Own occupation means you can file a claim if you are unable to work in your usual occupation or chosen field of employment. For instance, you would want an "own occupation" policy if you were a surgeon. If you were injured and could no longer perform surgery, you could "go on a claim", whereas if you had an "any occupation" policy, you would not necessarily qualify for benefits. The next definition is the **elimination period**.

The **elimination period** refers to the amount of time a disability must last before your benefits begin. Try to think of this as the deductible, but instead of being a monetary deductible, it is a time period.

For instance, let's say your long-term disability (LTD) policy has a 90-day elimination period. A disability event would need to last 90 days before your long-term disability policy would pay a single penny. Again, all policies are different and have different elimination periods. Lengthening the elimination period and reducing the percentage of your income that the policy covers affects the premium amount.

Long term disability policies can be costly, but you won't think that if something happens and you need it. If you do decide to commit a portion of your monthly income to LTD insurance, coordinating it with your STD (I couldn't resist) policy at work, can provide you with a smooth transition from short term to long term, and smooth out any bumps your family finances by providing you with at least some of your income during your recovery.

Home, Auto, and Personal Liability

Home, auto, and personal liability insurance are often the first insurance products many of us are exposed to. We buy our first car and have to go out and get insurance. Often, nobody is guiding us to make sure we have the right coverage for us. As we get older our insurance needs change and so should your coverage. If you signed up for your state minimum coverage when you got your first car, that was likely the right amount to protect you when you don't have any assets, to begin with. However, as we grow our net worth, our families get bigger our liability coverage needs do go up with it. This chapter is going to describe the home, auto, and umbrella policies (personal liability umbrella) and describe how to read your policy and what all of it means. I am going to start with auto insurance.

Auto Insurance

Car insurance, you probably have it but don't understand most of it. You look at your car insurance and you see a number 100/300/100 and probably have no idea what that even means. Here is what that break down means. It means you have $100,000 in bodily injury per person including death, $300,000 bodily injury per accident, and $100,000 in property damage coverage. This is generally considered decent coverage when starting. It is well above many state minimum coverages and provides nice well-rounded liability and property damage coverage for someone with low net worth.

As you get older, make more money, have more assets to protect from lawsuits, it is a good idea to up these limits to 250/500/250. In addition to liability and property damage, you will have some kind of limit for medical payments to others on your policy. It varies by the insurance carrier, but they go from $1,000 up to $25,000 at some carriers. I recommend having $10,000. When you are in an accident, this is the first thing the ambulance-chasing attorney wants to know about your insurance coverage. Many companies now offer towing/roadside assistance as well as rental reimbursement coverage if you need a rental car. What I have just described is full coverage insurance.

Some people opt to have liability only if they drive a beater and own the car outright. I don't recommend this unless you don't have any assets to lose or the money to afford full coverage. Having liability only will provide you no money if you are driving down the road and hit a deer and total your car. You are on foot or have to buy a new car with cash.

Concerning deductibles, a deductible is an amount you pay out of pocket before the insurance carrier pays anything. Some people like low deductibles, because they don't have a ton of cash and wouldn't be able to pay much out of pocket if they had to file a claim with their insurance company. The higher your deductible, the lower your monthly insurance cost will be. When you agree to absorb a higher amount, the insurance company has less at stake. Here is an example. You have an accident and have a $5,000 claim. If you have a $1,000 deductible, you pay the first $1,000 and the insurance company will pay $4,000. Remember, higher deductibles mean lower monthly payments. Having a nice emergency fund enables you to keep insurance deductibles high, to reduce monthly out of pocket. Insurance that has to be paid for even if you never use it, may as well cost as little as possible. That is a pretty basic overview of auto insurance, now let's look at homeowner's insurance.

Homeowner's Insurance

Just like your auto insurance protects you from accidents, your homeowner's insurance does the same thing, just on your home. Homeowners insurance differs in that there are several different kinds of coverage and the coverage follows you off of your property to wherever you are. The first part of home insurance is the coverage for the structure of the home itself. This part of the policy pays to repair or rebuild your home in case of fire, hurricane, hail, lightning, or other disaster listed in your policy. It does not pay for damage caused by flood, earthquake, or normal wear and tear. Most standard policies also cover structures that are not attached to your house directly, such as a garage, shed, or gazebo.

Next, you have coverage for personal belongings. Furniture, clothes, and other personal items are covered if they are stolen or destroyed by fire or another insured disaster. Most insurance carriers set this limit somewhere between 50-70% of the value of the structure of a home. This coverage also includes things that are off the premises, such as things in off-site storage, but can also cover them anywhere in the world. Items like jewelry, cash, guns, and silverware are covered, but they have low limits, so if you want to cover them for their full value, you have to add an endorsement to insure those items for their appraised value. Trees, plants, and shrubberies (even the ones from Roger the Shrubber) are also covered under a standard policy. Only some of you will get that last joke. The covered perils are theft, fire, lightning, explosion, vandalism, riot, and even falling aircraft.

The next part of the policy is your liability protection. Liability covers against lawsuits for bodily injury or property damage that the policyholder or a family member causes to other people. It also pays for injury caused by your pets, in some cases. Some dogs are excluded, but you will have to check with your insurance carrier for that. The liability coverage pays for both the cost of defending you court, as well as any court awards up to the policy limit. This liability coverage follows you anywhere in the world. Liability protection starts at $100,000 on homeowners and goes up to $500,000 with some carriers. That is the basics of homeowner's insurance, now let's take a look at an umbrella policy.

Personal Liability Umbrella

A personal liability umbrella policy provides additional liability coverage over and above coverage you carry on your auto, home, and boat, etc. Most of the aforementioned policies have limits of liability up to $500,000. However, if you injure someone seriously, you can blow through those limits just in medical bills and lost wages. If a judgment is made against you for more than your coverage, you will end up paying any excess amount out of your assets and/or future income.

An umbrella policy has three major benefits. First, $1 million or more of additional liability protection above your policy limits, additional coverage for legal defense, and coverage for many lawsuits your primary insurance does not cover (i.e. car rental coverage abroad, serving on non-profit boards, etc.).

Because it is so easy to cause someone serious injury where you are sued for more than your basic coverage it is smart for everyone to have an umbrella. In particular, those that have significant assets or income, good future potential, or anyone who stands to inherit sizable assets. In my opinion, if you are in the middle class, you should and can afford a $1 million umbrella, they are inexpensive on an annual basis ($150 to $250 per year). You want an umbrella policy that covers as much of your life activities as possible, especially those activities that are not covered by your basic insurance policies. Essentially, you want an umbrella liability policy with the fewest exclusions.

Estate Planning

"If you'll not settle for anything less than your best, you will be amazed at what you can accomplish in your lives." Vince Lombardi

Estate planning is not the most interesting topic for most people, and quite frankly, insurance can be downright boring. However, the downright boring things are often the most important things for you to get a handle on first. Why, because as previously mentioned they **form the foundation of your solid planning**. Don't assume because I have put them near the end of the book, it makes them less important. The fact is, the opposite is true. I just know these things are at the bottom of everyone's to-do list, and since I wanted you to read most of the book, I put them toward the end. You could have saved and budgeted for years, built up a nice portfolio of investments in the stock market and real estate, and failed to do this stuff and screw your heirs over royally by not taking the time to properly organize your estate planning. When I work with clients, this is often on their to-do list when they leave after my financial planning presentation, because most people have neglected to do it.

There are five basic estate planning documents that the majority of the people reading this need to have in place. If you have a more complicated financial life, a special needs family member, or other circumstances outside of the everyday, you may have some additional items, but for most individuals and families, these will do. In no particular order, the documents are an advance directive, durable power of attorney for health care, revocable living trust, a will, durable financial power of attorney. So, here we go.

Advance Directive

Advance directives are legal documents that provide instructions about your healthcare in case you are unable to speak for yourself. In my home state of Ohio, do not resuscitate orders, living wills, organ donation and durable powers of attorney are advance directives that are authorized under Ohio law.

Only about 1/3 of American adults have an advanced care plan in writing. This is concerning because some studies suggest that roughly 70% of Americans will be unable to make decisions for themselves at some point in their lives. This is why advanced care planning is important and it is not just important for the elderly or those with severe illness. Health care crisis can happen to anyone at any time. Any person over the age of 18 who can make his or her own decisions can complete an advance directive. You do not need a lawyer to complete it advanced directive, however, the forms need to be signed by a notary or two witnesses. The witness may include anyone except your physician, family members, or the person(s) you're naming as decision-maker in the advance directive.

**Now, just because you can do something without an attorney does not mean you should. If you are sitting down to get the rest of the legal documents completed, just get your advance directive done at the same time. The next item is a durable power of attorney for healthcare.

Durable Power of Attorney for Healthcare

A durable power of attorney for healthcare is a legal document that allows you to name someone else to make decisions about your health care in case you are not able to make those decisions yourself.

You have the right to decide what kind of medical treatment you do and do not want. If you have some specific wishes about your health care, a durable power of attorney for health care will ensure those wishes are honored even if you are physically or mentally unable to tell your doctors what you want.

If you do not have a durable power of attorney for health care and are physically or mentally unable to tell your doctors what you want, the following people in order of priority are legally authorized to make your healthcare decisions for you. A court-appointed guardian or conservator, your spouse or domestic partner, your adult child, an adult sibling, a close friend, or the nearest living relative.

To make a durable power of attorney for health care you sign a paper saying that you want a certain person or persons called your "agents" to make health care decisions for you if you are unable to make those decisions for yourself. So, what kind of decisions can my agent make you ask? Your agent can make a wide range of health care decisions including some of the following things. Whether to admit or discharge you from a hospital or nursing home. Which treatments or medications you do or do not want to receive, and who has access to your medical records. Your agent can only make these decisions if you cannot do so yourself and your agent must follow your wishes when making these decisions.

How will your agent know what you want? Well, you are going to put it in writing. You're going to state when you do or do not want your doctors to use machines to keep you alive. You're probably also going to put in there whether or not you want to be hooked up to feeding tubes that provide you with food and water. You'll probably include in there how you want your body disposed of when you die. Organ donation decisions and you'll name the person you want to be your legal guardian if necessary.

You can choose anyone over the age of 18 who you want to be your agent other than your doctor or other health care provider. Your agent can be a family member a friend. You should choose someone you can trust and who will carry out your wishes and not their own. You should discuss your wishes with your agent or agents and be sure the person you choose is willing to make decisions for you even if doing so may be difficult or upsetting for them. Ok, so we have talked about advance directives and healthcare power of attorney, now on to a revocable living trust.

Revocable Living Trust

A living trust is a special kind of trust that can own your stuff while you're still alive. A living trust spells out how to distribute what is in the trust after the owner dies. Almost anything can go in a living trust; real estate, bank accounts, vehicles, jewelry, as well as virtual items, like intellectual property.

When a living <u>trust is formed, the owner (grantor) transfers ownership of their assets to the trust itself.</u> So, let's pretend you own some kind of investment property. You can scratch off your name and put the name of the trust as owner. It is not that simple, but you get the point. The trust is now the owner of that property. You can do the same thing with other forms of property.

Next, you the grantor names a **"trustee"** and this person makes sure the instructions in the trust are carried out. As the title suggests some trusts are revocable and some are not. A **revocable trust** can be changed after it is executed. A revocable trust is the most common kind of trust by far, and you have some flexibility. An **irrevocable trust** is one that <u>can't</u> be changed even by the grantor of the trust.

There are some advantages and disadvantages to a revocable living trust. The advantages are they save time and money in the probate process; the trustee can immediately take care of end-of-life affairs. It offers more protection if challenged. A living trust is less likely to be challenged in court than a simple will. Finally, it protects your privacy better. A will is a public document, and anyone can get a copy of it. With a trust, no one can know the details without the trustee sharing that information.

Not everything is rainbows and unicorns with a living trust. First, there is the personal inconvenience. <u>You technically no longer own the property you assign to the trust.</u> If you want to sell something, you have to contact the trustee to take it out of the trust before you can sell it. Next, the attorney fees. Trusts can be costly to set up because you can't do one without an attorney. They can cost a couple of thousand dollars to set up. Last, the re-title and re-deed process. Once the trust is set up, all the assets going into the trust have to be re-titled and re-deeded with the trust as owner.

There are some great reasons to set up a trust but do so after wise counsel from a trusted attorney. Attorneys are fiduciaries and must act in your best interest, so if they are truly acting in your best interest, and they think a trust is necessary, you can trust the advice.

One final thought here. If you own property outside of your home state, then a living trust is necessary regardless of where the property is located. If not, your heirs will have to go through the ancillary probate process and that will not be fun for anyone. Now on to the will.

<u>**Wills**</u>

You probably have seen in movies the scene where family members gather in the lawyer's office as he or she reads the last will and testament of the deceased family where they tell them who gets what. In most of these movies, there is a greedy relative after the rich relative's wealth. Most of these scenes from Hollywood are not like real life. Normal people don't use their will to manipulate friends and family. There are several kinds of wills, but for this, we are just talking about the last will and testament. A will is a legally binding document that describes exactly how you want your assets like your property and other things you own to be handled after your death.

It can be as big as dividing up the family farm among five siblings, or something like giving someone your coin collection. A will protects the people and things you love the most. They are protected because you have made advanced plans which can give you peace of mind and because your loved ones won't have to deal with all the crazy things that can happen if you die without a will, called dying "**intestate**."

There are a few things a will should cover. There should be an executor. The executor carries out your written instructions and makes sure they get carried out. They'll read the will and carry out all other end-of-life business the way you wanted. You might hire a lawyer to do this, but they are usually an immediate family member. An adult child or close family friend will do, but I suggest you talk to them first, so they are not sideswiped with it after your death.

You are also going to name beneficiaries. These are the people that get your stuff, and they are usually immediate family members, but not always. They can be friends or charities you want to support. If you are married, you typically name your spouse as the sole beneficiary, especially if you have lots of shoes (gong). It is a good idea to name who gets what so there is no infighting. You'd be surprised out how nasty some people get over stuff, otherwise known as nonsense. If you don't, there could be a family feud over your golf clubs or your cat fluffy. If you are single without kids, you will most likely name your family members, friends, or charities as beneficiaries.

If you have minor children or a child with a special need(s), you will likely name guardians for those children as part of your will. It will name who will take care of them if you and your spouse pass away together. You will also want to name who gets your pets. Pet care is easier than raising children, but it is an important consideration. Those are some of the things a will does cover, but what doesn't it cover.

Things a will doesn't cover

A will can tell your family what to do with your tennis racket and your coin collection, but it can't tell what to do with retirement funds like your 401k or IRA's, life insurance, or joint tenancy assets (something you own with your spouse). Those items pass by a named beneficiary, or in the case of jointly owned property by automatic transfer to the survivor.

Durable Financial Power of Attorney

A durable power of attorney for finances, or financial power of attorney is a simple, inexpensive way to arrange for someone to manage your finances if you become incapacitated. A financial power of attorney is an excellent document for you but can also be a blessing for your family. If you become unable to decide for yourself and you haven't prepared a durable power of attorney, a court proceeding is probably inescapable. Your spouse, close relatives, or companion will have to ask the court for authority over at least some of your financial affairs.

A financial power of attorney can be drafted so that it goes into effect as soon as you sign it. You should specify that you want your financial power of attorney to be <u>durable</u>. If you don't, in some states it will automatically end if you later become incapacitated. You can also specify when you want the power of attorney to go into effect, such as a doctor certifies that you have become incapacitated. This is often called a <u>"springing" durable power of attorney</u> and allows you to stay in control unless and until a certain event takes place. Be aware, these can sometimes cause delays and problems for the person you name as your agent or in some states an attorney.

It is pretty common for people to give their agent broad power to handle all of your financial affairs so choose wisely. You can give your agent as much or as little power as you want them to have. The agent is required to act in your best interest and keep accurate records, keep your property separate from theirs, and avoid conflicts of interest.

Your durable power of attorney automatically ends at your death. That means, your agent does not have powers to handle your financial affairs after your death unless that person is also your executor. Your durable power of attorney ends only if you revoke it, you get a divorce (in some not all states), a court invalidates your document, or your agent is no longer available.

Taxes

"Whatever you do, don't do it half way." Bob Beamon

I know what you are thinking. What could be more boring than taxes? I know but taxes are a huge part of our life whether we want to admit it or not, so taking some time to think about your taxes while you are saving, and investing is as important as any other planning decision you will make.

Many people see their taxes as an issue they need to address only at the end of the year, and they are either doing their return or paying someone to do it for them. Most of the time, they are getting zero advice about whether they need to make changes or not. The return is filed, they get a huge tax return and in almost every case the money gets spent on something of little value. This chapter is about looking at your taxes as an ongoing process that can be planned throughout the year to minimize the amount of tax you send to the IRS using the tax code. Smart steps you can take, which keeps more money in your pocket during the year instead of giving it to the Government to use all year for zero percent interest.

It is my job to advise people on smart financial decisions that benefit them. I also do taxes as part of my practice. I have spent my life up to this point serving my Country first, and now the community I live in by offering the kind of advice many people need because money is confusing for some people. I take great pride in staying on top of the latest information in financial planning and I notice a theme when I talk with people every day. **They do not understand their taxes.** I have been doing taxes since I got my first job as a paperboy in 1988. Back then, we got the forms from the library and filled them out by hand. Nowadays, a computer program and ten or fifteen minutes and you're done. If you overpay on your taxes during the year and don't use all of your deductions and tax credits, guess what, you just gave the IRS more money for no reason because you overpaid, to begin with, and then failed to get it all back. Does that sound like a wise strategy to you? It sure doesn't to me.

At least once a week I ask a potential client what they are doing to invest for retirement and they say, "I don't have the money to invest." My next question is how much their tax return is each year, and they proudly say with a huge grin "I usually get back $3,500." Naturally, I ask them if they got any interest from the IRS for loaning them that much money? I normally get a blank stare because they don't understand the question. I am sorry, but some math is in order in this chapter, but I hope to keep you awake, so I will do this fast.

Let's say with some smart tax planning you decide not to give the IRS your free $3,500 per year but instead keep it for yourself and pay just what you owe. You take the extra $291.67 per month and invest it in the market ($3,500/12 = $291.67). With an 8% interest rate for the year, you will end with $3,655 at the end of year one buy using the money you have been giving away each year for nothing. Now, do that for 35 years and you will have north of $733,000 in an IRA. That was a very simple example because it does not factor in the additional tax savings involved in deferring income in a tax-deductible IRA now, future pay raises which may increase future contributions. You would be surprised at how many people do this every year though. The very people that tell me they can't afford to save and invest do this kind of poor tax planning.

Planning Your Tax Bracket for Retirement

Tax planning for retirement is also very important because of the way the current tax code treats tax-deferred, taxable, and tax-free retirement accounts, we have a tremendous amount of flexibility in how we save and where we save from a tax standpoint. The problem is that many people do not take advantage of all that is available to them concerning this kind of planning either. Almost half, (46%) of recent retirees wish they had planned better for handling taxes in retirement, according to a new survey from Nationwide Retirement Institute, and 1 in 4 retirees reports paying thousands of dollars more in taxes in retirement than they thought they would.

Gaining an understanding during your accumulation years of how your retirement income will be taxed gives you a tremendous advantage over retirees that wait until they are retired to learn of the tax implications. I want to educate all retirement savers on the need to think about how each retirement account plays a part in positioning your retirement dollars, so you pay as little tax as necessary when you switch from saving for retirement to spending down your retirement accounts. Every dollar you have to pay in taxes is one less dollar you get to spend on yourself in retirement. One less vacation you take, one less experience, and less to pass on to your heirs.

Pre-retirees are starting to find out there is a tax-bomb waiting for them once they retire. What is worse, is when they find out that the tax bomb **could have been avoided** if they had done some retirement income planning. To plan for this, you need some knowledge about how the tax bomb gets created in the first place and proper steps to take to properly reduce your tax liability.

Many people think when they retire, their taxes will naturally decrease. No longer working equals lower taxes in many people's minds. Most people spend their entire working lives saving money in their tax-deferred 401k or Traditional IRA. These are wonderful plans, and give tax savings today, but they kick the specter of tax-deferred income down the road to when you retire. Things become problematic when you are forced to take money out of these accounts at 72 years old.   That is the age when required minimum distributions (RMD) kick in. In other words, you are forced to take money out because the IRS has been patiently waiting on their money. It does not matter if you need the money or not, you **have** to take the money out and it is recognized as ordinary income. If you miss an <u>RMD</u>, there is a 50% penalty on the amount you should have taken out.

The real kicker to your retirement income is your Social Security benefit. You can start your SS payments as early as 62, but some planning here as well can build delayed retirement credits which will increase your SS benefit. At age 70 you must take SS benefits. Which could probably be a book by itself. As you are probably starting to see, you will have streams of income, all coming in at the same time. All of these income streams coming in can spell, as Travis Tritt would say T-R-O-U-B-L-E.

What a lot of people fail to plan for is the taxation of their Social Security. Most people believe that SS is a tax-free benefit, but that is just not the case. For a lot of people, it is true, but once you pass some very low-income thresholds, the IRS can tax up to 85% of your SS benefits. The fact of the matter is, with a little pre-planning this tax bomb can be avoided for many people. Once you pass the age of 70, the ability to reduce taxes greatly diminishes. A lot of people will begin retiring in their 60's, which is great for advanced tax planning.

If you retire in your 60's your income will most likely drop significantly, and you drop into a lower tax bracket. Think of the tax brackets as something you move through as your professional life advances. When you are young you are at the lower end and as your career advances, you move up into the higher tax brackets. When you are in your 40's and 50's you are likely in the highest bracket you will ever be in. At this level, you don't want any retirement tax planning, because you are trying to defer as much as possible to reduce taxes now. Once you retire, and your income drops, you may fall back to the 12% tax bracket. Now that you have all these assets built up, and you are in the lower tax bracket, it is time to jump into tax planning to take full advantage of the lower tax brackets early in your retirement. I call this, your retirement tax planning window and it goes anywhere from 62 to 70 depending on when you push the retirement button.

There are three types of accounts to put your assets in. Always taxable, taxed later, and never taxed. Always taxable are accounts like bank accounts, money markets, and a standard non-IRA investment account (well, sometimes it depends on the investments held in the account). Tax-deferred accounts which include your 401k at work and traditional IRA, tax-deferred annuity. Never taxable accounts are a Roth 401k or Roth IRA.

Now that you have a basic understanding of all the moving parts, you can begin to tax plan for retirement. There are some things you can do to reduce your taxes and we are going to talk about those now.

First, you can convert money in an always taxable account to a never taxable account. Commonly referred to as Roth conversion, this allows you to pay tax now while you are in a lower tax bracket thus removing money from your always taxable and putting it into your never taxable account. This strategy reduces your future required minimum distributions because they will not be required in your never taxable account, under the current tax code.

Let's work through an example so you can see how this would work in real life. In 2020 you retired at 62 and get $50,000 in ordinary income. Assume you have $500,000 in your traditional IRA, which is taxed later. You are married and your tax filing status is married filing jointly with your spouse. In 2020 the standard deduction for married filing jointly is $24,800 giving you $30,250 to convert to your Roth IRA and still keep you in the 12% tax bracket. Doing this every year, while in the lower tax bracket enables you to move a sizable sum into never taxable and thus minimizing future taxes in retirement. Converting money from a taxed later account to a never taxable account and staying in your lower tax bracket is the first step to plan for taxes in retirement.

The best way to help yourself is to create tax diversification while you are still young. Most people end up with large sums in their taxed later accounts because the world defaults to the 401k. If you are saving money in a 401k, you should be thinking of saving some in the Roth 401k option inside your plan or open a Roth IRA outside of the 401k and begin saving there. If you are already maxing out both and want to do more, then put money away into an always taxable account. This kind of tax diversification will give you more options down the road and a variety of accounts to withdrawal your retirement income from to give you maximum flexibility and allows **YOU** to engineer your tax rate in your retirement years.

A lot of retirees are surprised by their tax bill. Every dollar you send them is less you get to use and enjoy. However, if you take advantage of your tax planning window, you can reduce your future tax burden and keep more of your hard-saved dollars. Trust me, you will thank me down the road when Social Security kicks in and you can shuck and jive the taxman.

Something that is becoming known as **tax-alpha** is starting to emerge and it is a way to measure the value of the tax-focused planning can do. Without tax-focused planning, advisors, tax preparers, and clients are making costly mistakes. Taxpayers who merely drop off their file at their tax preparers office or use some off the shelf software miss tax-saving opportunities. Accountants who limit their client engagements to tax preparation limit their clients' ability to reduce their clients' tax exposure until it is too late. Financial planners who advise on investments, retirement planning, and education savings but don't do any tax planning lead their clients down a road towards higher tax liability than would be realized with some smart tax planning.

<u>Taxes might be the most important issue facing you now and in retirement</u>. People who don't plan well will pay more in tax and have less money to use for themselves due to inefficient tax strategies with their retirement income. This is an area where the expertise of a tax professional will save you more money than you will ever pay them to do this kind of planning. When I work with my clients, these are the kinds of things we are talking about year in and year out. If your advisor does not, I suggest you find a tax professional that can advise you now and in the future on this very important topic.

Financial Health & Physical Wellbeing

"Simplicity is the ultimate sophistication." Loa Tzu

Have you ever heard the saying "health is wealth" or maybe this one "you spend your whole life working for money and the rest of your life spending your money trying to get your health?" There is some scientific evidence that financial problems do affect your health in a variety of ways, and we are going to explore them, so we have some additional motivation for taking care of our finances.

Researchers are finding more and more <u>connections between your finances and your health.</u> With symptoms that go far beyond stress. In our society, we have tripled our debt since the 1980s. Heart disease, stroke, and mental illness are all on the rise, and finances seem to be partly to blame. Thanks to the amount of attention financial wellness have gotten over the last several years, folks are waking up to the realization that paying down debt, improving your credit score, and building more savings have the effect of improving your overall health.

<u>So how do finances affect physical health?</u>

Part of an overall wellness program should include taking great care of your financial health and ensuring you set yourself up for a prosperous future. I am going to go through a few ways poor money management can manifest itself physically in your life.

The first way financial problems can manifest in your physical health is raised diastolic blood pressure. High blood pressure is a precursor to a host of health problems, including heart attacks and strokes. A 2013 study from Northwestern University showed adults 24-32 who had high debt had higher diastolic blood pressure. Aside from money issues, this age group should be in optimal health. The next medical issue associated with debt is increased muscular tension.

Muscle tension, including back pain, was reported by over half of those with high debt loads. Additionally, 44% had migraines or other headaches compared to 15% without debt stress. If you believe you are suffering from tension due to money problems, consider making a financial plan and adding some physical activity to reduce stress and improve your overall health.

Digestive issues are another issue identified with increased debt stress. The digestive system is often referred to as the center of health, so when under heavy financial stress many people don't follow regular eating habits. Healthy foods may not even be accessible or affordable for those in financial trouble. 27% of people with high debt stress reported ulcers or other digestive issues, compared to 8% without.

The last section of health-related issues was pretty much all about physical problems related to financial dysfunction, but what mental health issues can this type of financial stress cause? Money is so much more than paper, plastic, or online accounts. For many, it represents their ability to feed their family, get an education, or improve the overall quality of life. When your financial health is poor, the psychological impacts can be just a debilitating as the physical. The feeling of failure or doubt has the potential of turning into a mental illness.

Financial problems can cause depression, which can lead to poor work performance, tardiness, and eventually the loss of your job. The feelings of despair are pretty common. One study found 23% of those with debt reported having severe depression to just 4% without.

Increased anxiety is also common among those that carry heavy debt loads. 29% of adults with debt suffer severe anxiety compared to 4% without. The feelings of anxiety and panic caused by financial stress can be the springboard for an all-around unhealthy lifestyle. 55% of adults in lower-income households say they handle stress through a sedentary lifestyle or unhealthy habits like watching TV, drinking alcohol, smoking, and stress eating. The uncertainty of being able to pay one's bills can keep them in a state of panic and fear.

Finally, the feeling of shame and embarrassment. 35% of Americans are embarrassed to admit they have too much credit card debt, and 43% said they would feel judged if family and friends found out. That shame can lead to isolation, which can lead back to mental health issues and an unhealthy lifestyle.

As with most hardships in life, there can be light at the end of the tunnel. When you reduce debt, put money in savings, and have something set aside for a rainy day it has a very calming effect. Your mind begins to be freed to focus on other things, and your body may begin to heal too. Not only that, you may get a boost to your self-esteem. 81% of people surveyed said they found their other goals easier to achieve when their finances were in order. Confidence turns on like a light switch in many cases and you find that things that seemed undoable are now within your reach. **I know this because I have lived it.**

When you get financially healthy, the physical problems you experienced, will likely improve. According to Carole Stovall, a phycologist in Washington says "When people pay off debt, they're going to say 'my stomach feels better, my heart feels better.'" Adding to that, 69% of people agreed if they had the money, they would eat better.

A life well-lived consists of finances well managed. While there are many things you can do to improve your physical and mental health, there's no denying the science behind health and finances. If you do everything in your power to stay out of debt, build short-term and long-term savings you'll most likely reap the rewards both physically and mentally.

I encourage you to reach out to someone, a trusted member of the family, or a friend to seek assistance with getting back to financial health if your finances have gotten away from you. If not, go to a financial counselor who can help you without judgment get yourself on the right track financially.

In Real Life

"If you do what you've always done, you'll get what you've always gotten." Tony Robbins

Before I finish, I wanted to go through what all of this will look like in real life as you navigate your household finances on your way to wealth and prosperity. Jerry decided a career as a plumber looked way more appealing than going to college out of high school and he got hired as an apprentice plumber making $14 per hour while learning the trade. Being only 18 years old, he still lives at home while he saves money and builds his skills.

Jerry's girlfriend Tammy is going to the local community college taking the two-year surgical technician program. She is also living at home with her parents, so she can save on living expenses and works part-time answering phones at an insurance agency. She gets $10 per hour and it gives her a chance to study when the phones are not ringing. By going to the community college, it cuts down costs for her education which limits her need for student loans.

Jerry and Tammy both have cars that are paid for and they have the state minimum auto coverage on them because they are both still young and are not protecting much in the way of assets, well they don't have any.

Three years have passed, and Jerry and Tammy are looking at getting married. They are still driving the cars they had three years ago, neither has accumulated much credit card debt, and they want to start saving for their first home. Jerry is now a journeyman plumber where he works, and he makes $45,000 per year, has a 401k plan, and health benefits. Tammy got hired at the big hospital in town working in the operating room. She has been there a year and has already gotten a pay raise. She makes $46,000 and health benefits, 401k, and short-term disability insurance.

They recently read an awesome book by this guy named Jim Kilgore, so they know they should only look at homes that are 3 times their gross annual income. They are looking at homes no bigger than what they need, with the idea of having 2 kids someday. They opt for a three-bedroom ranch in their hometown and their absolute max is $273,000 homes and under. Which is perfect, because that is above the average price in the area they live in. They find a nice 3-bedroom bath and a half for $160,000 with a big back yard and nice 2 car detached garage in addition to the one car attached garage.

They have both been diligently saving because they stayed at home up to this point and didn't have to pay rent in addition to having great jobs. Without student loan debt or car payments, they have saved a combined $48,000 in savings. They will have plenty to put down on the house and a cash buffer in savings after closing costs and everything. After making the 20% down payment, they take out a mortgage for $128,000. All in with taxes and homeowner's insurance their house payment is $739.65 per month. Their housing cost ratio is 9.2% well below my recommendation of no more than 30% of monthly gross income. Because they had so much saved for their house purchase, they already have 6 months of expenses in liquid savings in case of a global pandemic.

Neither Jerry nor Tammy are extravagant people and they have decided not to have a huge wedding with horses, chariots, or the giant reception. They decided it was more important to have their house and a small wedding with just close family and a nice honeymoon cruise.

They started working on a monthly budget together, so they can get in the habit of living within their means and using their company-sponsored retirement plans to start saving for retirement. Because they did so well selecting their house, they have a lot of disposable income to put towards their savings and investing goal. They decide that come hell or high water they are going save 15% of their monthly income every month. 3% in their company-sponsored 401k plans because that is the maximum match. The other 9% will be split into his and hers Roth IRA's. $1,200 per month will be split between Jerry and Tammy 401k's at work, Roth IRAs for both of them, and the rest if any will go into a regular brokerage account. The breakdown will look like this, roughly $115 per month is going into their 401k plans where their employer matches their contribution, I mean why not take the free money, right? Each will be maxing their Roth IRA contributions with after-tax money for tax-free growth and tax-free withdrawals years down the road.

Now that they have moved and gotten married, they both seek out the assistance of an insurance professional to help guide them in getting some term life insurance in place in case something bad happens and they name each other as beneficiaries. They each get a 30-year term policy with a $500,000 death benefit for $35 per month and while they are at it, Mike their insurance guy recommends they up the coverage on their home and auto to appropriate levels for their income and assets. They increase the coverage to 100/300/100 on their cars with towing and rental coverage and $300,000 in personal liability on their homeowner's policy.

Mike, the insurance guy recommends an estate attorney that will assist Jerry and Tammy with getting all of their estate planning documents in place for a reasonable fee. Tom, their attorney helps Jerry and Tammy get their advance directive, healthcare powers of attorney, wills, as well as durable financial powers of attorney in place. Jerry and Tammy feel very confident knowing they have made some really smart choices with their finances and now they have the protection in place in case something horrible happens to one of them. Tom makes sure to let them know any time they have a major life change to give him a call to make sure nothing needs updating. He explains things like having children, getting an inheritance will be things he will want to know about to update their estate planning. They are happy to have an attorney looking out for this stuff for them because they don't understand it very much.

As the year winds down, it is time for Jerry and Tammy to go see their tax preparer. Bob completes their tax return for them and advises them he thinks they need to make some changes to their income tax withholding because they are getting too much back from the IRS. He tells them which changes to make and magically, they are getting $162 per month more in take-home pay, which is great because Tammy needs a new car. Her car has been to the shop twice in the last six months and Jerry wants Tammy to have reliable transportation due to her 20-minute commute downtown each day. She opts to go with a Kia Forte because with a very small down payment the monthly car payment is only $223 per month. With the tax savings, their tax preparer Bob just found, they are only spending $61 net out of pocket more than they were before Bob helped them make their adjustments. Because their monthly cash flow is so positive, the insurance premium increase on the new car hardly makes a dent. They bring home $7,600 after tax and a solid budget, they realize they have $2,500 extra every month in discretionary income.

They feel like they are putting enough in their investments and want to diversify into some small rental properties close to home. Jerry and Tammy decided to start taking $1,500 of their extra cash flow to put down on some multi-unit rentals close to home. For the next 18 months, they deposited $1,500 into their brokerage account where they accumulate enough to make a down payment on a 4-unit rental just down the road. They put down 20% on the 4-unit apartment complex listed for $278,000 and the 4-unit building has a positive cash flow of $527 per month that they put into an account in case of repairs. Once a year, they take a portion and put a lump sum towards principle.

Jerry is now a licensed plumber and decided to start his own plumbing company. Tammy is now a supervisor over several of the surgical techs in her department. They had their first child last year and as luck would have it barely a year later Tammy is pregnant with their second child. They both make better money they were making when they first got married, but their house is still plenty big for their growing family. Since they've had such positive cash flow, they have been able to update the roof, the kitchen, and both bathrooms in the last few years. Their liquid savings at the bank is plenty to get them through as Jerry starts his business, but they know most millionaires are business owners, so Jerry takes the leap of faith and uses some of their liquid savings to get his plumbing company off the ground.

Jerry takes the 401k assets from his previous employer and rolls them into a Traditional IRA. Now that he owns a business, he starts a retirement plan for his own business. He does not intend to grow and just wants to do service plumbing in the towns surrounding his own. In his first year in business, he does $122,000 in net income and puts a lump-sum in his newly established retirement plan of $15,000.

The kids are growing up and are in school. Jerry and Tammy meet with their insurance agent and attorney to update their insurance and estate planning documents now that their family has grown. Their investments and real estate holdings are growing steadily, and they want to make sure of adequate protection from lawsuits and asset transfer if something bad happened to one of them. Mike recommends they add an umbrella policy to add additional liability protection for their personal assets and they decide to place their real estate holdings in an LLC and separate them from their personal assets. Their net worth has grown significantly over the last few years, and since they got married went from negative net worth to $460,000 this year.

Jerry and tammy are now in their late thirties and the kids are teenagers. Jerry's plumbing company regularly does over $100,000 per year after expenses and he saves about $15,000 in his company retirement plan. They have acquired three more rentals and they all generate positive cash flow each month. Jerry and Tammy have now reached the point where they are aggressively paying the mortgages on each of the rentals to get them paid off. They plan to have all four rentals paid off in ten years, so the rent minus expenses can go right into their next investment opportunity. Their house is almost paid off, but Jerry wants a pool and an extra room added on, so they take out a home equity loan and add a beautiful room on the back of their house where they can watch football and entertain friends. They put in a swimming pool in the back yard, so the kids can have their friends over, and Jerry and Tammy can always be aware of who the kids hang out with.

Jerry and Tammy still sit down every month and do their budget together. At this point in their life, it only takes them about 30 minutes each month because they have been doing it for so long. They value the time they get to spend together working on their finances. They have never had a money fight. They decide it is time to start teaching the kids about money and investing and so next month, they will include their kids in the budget meeting.

Jerry gets a phone call that takes him to his knees. Tammy was on her way to work and she was in a horrible traffic accident and was severely injured. Tammy's legs were both broken in several places, she has three broken ribs, a cracked bone in her face, and a broken arm. Tammy is stable, but it will take her several months to recover. Jerry is just happy that she is ok, and that they chose the correct employee benefits through the hospital. Her short-term disability policy she has been paying for all these years will pay 60% of her monthly take-home while she recovers from her injuries.

Thanks to their savings and budgeting for all of these years, they have 2 years of monthly expenses in liquid savings, so there will be no problem as she recovers at home and Jerry hires someone to do the cleaning and some of the things around the house. The kids also pick up the slack, all the while they are just happy mom is ok.

The kids are now all grown up and have moved out of the house. Jerry and Tammy have a healthy net worth as they have continued to save and invest. All of the rental properties are now paid off and are generating monthly income as well. Jerry and Tammy have now paid off the home mortgage as well as the home equity loan on the house and now they own their house free and clear. Another plumbing company owner comes to Jerry and tells him he wants to retire and asks Jerry if he wants to buy his business.

Jerry and Tammy agree this is the investment opportunity they should take now that all of the rentals are paid off. The new plumbing company already has a journeyman working that runs most of the service calls already, so it is not much additional work for Jerry. Jerry does decide to hire an office manager to manage the daily schedule and run the day-to-day business. Jerry and Brian, the owner of the company Jerry is buying, structure a deal that allows Jerry to buy out Brian over the next 4 years. In four years, Jerry will own the new company all by himself.

Tammy and Jerry are now in their mid-fifties. Their net worth has gone up every year and now approaches $3,000,000 and their investment portfolio in the stock market is about $1,200,000 of that. Their tax professional they started with years ago is still in the business, and he works with them every year to advise them on their complicated tax situation. Bob is always looking for ways to help them save money on taxes just like he did back when they were first starting. Because they are getting closer to retirement, he is looking for ways to best position their retirement assets to enable them to have a great lifestyle but minimize taxes at the same time. Due to the recent business acquisition, Bob sees this as an opportunity with the extra business expenses they will have to do some additional tax planning.

He believes their tax bracket will go down for the next four years and he encourages them to make some Roth conversions from their traditional IRA assets to pay the taxes now while tax rates are lower and their tax bracket is lower for the next 4 years. Bob estimates this will save them hundreds of thousands of dollars in taxes in retirement by making these moves now.

After their annual review with their financial planner, Jerry and Tammy meet with their attorney, insurance professional, and accountant. Jim, their financial planner thinks Jerry can retire now and they can live comfortably off of what they have accumulated up to this point well into their 90's. Jerry and Tammy just turned 62 their investment portfolio is now worth over $2,000,000, they have the four rental properties paying $6,000 per month in monthly income for them, and the plumbing company has grown to the point Jerry is ready to sell and retire. Tammy will keep working until 65 to keep their insurance coverage and retire at 65 when they can go on Medicare.

Jerry hires a company to do a valuation of his plumbing business and they come back with a value of $1,200,000. After listing the company for sale with a business broker two interested buyers compete for buying Jerry's company. Jerry ends up getting an offer for $1,250,000 and they structure the deal so that over the next 10 years, Jerry will receive $125,000 per year. That $125,000 per year in income will take him to 72 years old when he has to start taking money from his IRA. The IRA can continue to grow for the next ten years before he starts taking from it. Because this more than covers Jerry and Tammy's annual living expenses they allow their Social Security to grow until both of their full retirement ages. They begin collecting at age 67 and a half and get $5,600 per month after they pay Medicare part B premium.

They continue to process Roth conversions each year just up to the next tax bracket to allow them to pull money out of their tax-deferred IRA and move it into their Roth (never taxed again IRA). These are strategic moves that help minimize taxes during the last few years before they have to take their required minimum distributions, which are still going to be substantial. At this point, they are making annual gifts to their children, and charities to help remove money from the IRAs and reduce the likelihood of taxation of their social security benefits and reduce the size of their estate. Their tax professional Bob is always looking out for them and tells them the estate tax exemption is due to revert to pre-tax cuts and jobs act levels in 2025, so reducing the amount of their estate is essential to eliminate the possibility of paying estate taxes at their death.

Jerry and Tammy talk to their estate planning attorney that helps them set up some estate planning strategies to set up trusts to help pass assets to the kids with the least amount of tax consequences.

Did you notice anything about Tammy and Jerry? Neither had a four-year college degree, but they worked hard and had a steady stream of income, lived within their means, diversified their investments, budgeted every month for their expenses, saved money for future investment opportunities, created passive income streams for themselves, and they did not have excessive debt. This example can be the life of anyone you know. Choices are what it boils down to. Choices which include self-discipline and delayed gratification. Choices that include being content with what you have and not seeking to keep up with the Joneses. They met with the professionals they chose to use to help them in this journey regularly and took their advice. Most of all, they followed the same process month in and month out over their entire career.

Now, you can take these numbers and make them larger or even smaller, but if you follow the same principles I have laid out in this book, there is no reason you can't end up in the same position as Jerry and Tammy did. Life will never be without adversity, as you can see Tammy almost died in a car accident. Your life will never be smooth sailing, you can count on that, but you can make your financial life pretty smooth if you follow these simple principles I have described in these pages.

Last thing before I wrap up. I believe with conviction everyone needs to have business professionals in their life to assist them in making wise financial decisions. The four professionals everyone needs on their team are as follows in no particular order. An insurance professional, an accountant, an attorney, and a fiduciary financial planner. Find professionals that act as fiduciaries for you, which means they have to look out for your best interest and not their own. Humbling yourself and taking the advice from people in these areas of your life will save you time, money, and frustration throughout your financial journey. Hire the best you can find and let them guide you along the way.

Concluding Thoughts

"It takes as much effort to wish as it does to plan." *Eleanor Roosevelt*

There is no doubt we have an issue with the lack of financial education and literacy in our society. It might even be intentionally built this way. If you think about it, when you take the fact that 70% of US gross domestic product (GDP) is made up of our consumption, and we are taxed at practically every turn, it starts to look like the cards are stacked against us.

A glimmer of hope begins to reveal itself when you realize it is your choices and not any other outside forces that are keeping you from reaching financial health and prosperity. I regularly teach people these sound financial principles and follow them on their journey to healthy finances. Your career choices, your debt choices, your savings and investing choices, your lifestyle choices, your behaviors are what matters most when reaching financial health and prosperity.

You have to decide what you want your financial path to look like this year, next year, the next ten years, and beyond. You get to choose! The smart financial principles I have laid out in this book, if applied in your life, will produce a life of happiness and wealth beyond what you ever thought possible. You simply have to give it time to happen. The society we live in is "Give it to me now and pay for it later."

Choosing to be different will ensure you have a different outcome. I want you to realize something though, you will be different from your friends and family. You will say things like, "It is not in the budget," and other people will give you a weird look. You will say things like, "Oh, we don't have credit card debt" and people will turn their heads like the girl in the Exorcist thinking they just saw Bigfoot. They will not understand why, and you can feel confident that you are in a better place than they are.

Many people out there are living their lives to impress others and they are drowning in debt because they just want to look the part. Look at social media, do you ever see someone putting all the bad stuff out there going on in their lives, or is it just the good stuff? People want their family and friends to believe something is not true, while their friends look at that and go wow, they have it together. The reality of the situation is probably drastically different than what is being portrayed. Cars, houses, boats, timeshares, and many other "things" are robbing people of true happiness because happiness is not found in things. Contentment is often found in the things that are free, more time with your family, free from the restraints of being chained to your job. Contentment is having the resources to cover any of life's challenges. Contentment is often found in helping others when the need arises and many other places than just stuff.

Free yourself from all of this by making different choices than everyone else. At the end of this book, I am going to put my 10 Indicators of Financial Health. Additionally, I will put links to all the resources I have mentioned in this book. Lastly, I ask you to please let me know what you think of the book by adding a review wherever you bought it. Thank you for taking the time to read it, and I truly appreciate your support. I will not wish you luck, because you don't need luck, you need intentional decisions to make financial health and prosperity a reality.

Appendix A

10 Indicators of Financial Health

1. A steady source of income

If you have a steady job, no matter the salary, you can decide to make all the rest of these items below a priority. A steady source of income gives you the ability to do everything else below here. Businesses need positive cash flow to be profitable and households need positive cash flow to stay healthy.

2. Emergency Fund

Save $1,000 in your savings account and leave it there for nothing except a financial emergency. Never be tempted to spend it on nonsense. Having this buffer will enable you to absorb most of life's curveballs without putting on a credit card. If you do have an emergency that exceeds your emergency fund, then you are only putting a small portion on a credit card to fill in the gap. Pay this off and then get your $1,000 emergency fund built back up for the next curveball.

3. 3-6 months of expenses

Once you have your $1,000 emergency fund, work to save 3-6 months of your living expenses in case you get laid off, have a short-term disability situation or some other unforeseen event takes place. When you have 3-6 months of expenses in savings, you can relax and not panic. This takes the stress out of a lay off or short-term disability event. If your job provides short-term disability insurance, you will have the savings to fill in the gap and this will likely last longer than 6 months with some disability insurance benefit.

4. Little to no debt

Debt puts you in a position of indentured servanthood. It
means you eliminate or seriously limit your financial
flexibility by taking on too much debt. When you put too
much on credit cards and allow the balances to balloon, you
have robbed your future self by bringing forward future
earnings to today. Avoid revolving debt at all costs and make
sure you keep your home and car purchases prudent. A
Mercedes when a Ford Focus would do is just silly.

5. Savings and investments

Having money in money markets/liquid savings gives you
the ability to make investments when the opportunity
presents itself. I can't tell you how many investment
opportunities have passed people by because they simply
didn't have the money to invest when the opportunity
presented itself.

6. Passive Income

Start building streams of passive income. This can be in
dividend-paying stocks, real estate investments, or other
streams of income that take little to no effort to produce
additional income streams. You should aim for seven streams
of income.

7. Long term thinking

Making long term plans will give your brain the motivation it
needs to bring plans to reality. Thinking long term gives your
mind focus and brings all of your other financial decisions
back to your long-term plans fit into every decision. Giving
yourself a target to hit helps organize your thoughts and
actions to enable you to hit that target, no matter how far off
in the distance it seems.

8. Budget for expenses

Every financially successful person I know uses a budget for
their household expenses. Telling your money where to go,
including savings and investments, ensures you are allocating
your household cashflow wisely each month. Sitting down
with your spouse each month and creating your monthly
budget creates accountability between you and improves
martial communication, and what married couple doesn't
need more of that.

9. Life-long learning

Commit to life-long learning. This can be reading a book each
week in different areas that you are not familiar with, or
industry-specific to the career you are in. It can also be
expanding your skill set by taking classes in an area you are
unfamiliar with. An example could be taking some
accounting classes at the local community college or studying
for a new certification in your chosen field.

10. Contentment

I can't stress this last point enough, learning to be content with
what you have will make all the difference in the world.
Ignoring the constant advertising you are exposed to and
being happy with the life you have, not the life you neighbor
has put you in a position to do all the other 9 on this list.

Resources

On my website, I have included several Excel spreadsheets to assist you in your journey to financial health and prosperity.

Go to www.thebuckeyefinanceguy.com and you can download the following resources.

1. Budgeting Form-A monthly budget planner to complete at the end of each month for the next month.

2. Personal Monthly Budget-An expanded version of the budgeting form, but with the entire year in mind.

3. Financial Goals Worksheet-A spreadsheet to write down your SMART financial goals and put them in motion.

4. Debt Reduction Calculator-This calculator lets you select the strategy you want to use to pay off your debt. Lowest balance or highest interest rate and gives you the payoff schedule.

5. Net-Worth Calculator-It is important to keep track of your net worth each year. This spreadsheet helps you do that.